WESTERN PROFESSIONALISM
BENGALI ROOTS

The Global Bengali's Guide to International Success

RASEL KHAN

Book Design by HMDPublishing.com

Published by: Independent Publishing Network
ISBN: 978-1-80605-181-6

Imprint: Independently published

DEDICATED TO

My late parents and countless teachers,
who helped me to keep an open mind

THANKS TO

Kazi Mahjabeen
Ashiqur Rahman
Joshim Uddin
Rausan Khanam
Prosen Ghosh
Nila Warda
Kazi Arefin Ahmed
Stacey K

And some really special friends

ABOUT THE AUTHOR

Rasel Khan has spent the last twenty-eight years navigating the complex, ever changing world of global projects with a blend of strategic insight, leadership finesse, and just enough cultural savvy to make magic happen across time zones.

Based in the United Kingdom, Rasel has led everything from tight knit teams to sprawling multinational groups. Whether managing a dozen developers in Dhaka or steering high stakes launches across Europe and North America, his superpower lies in adapting to diverse cultural dynamics while keeping teams aligned, inspired, and moving forward. He frequently recruits team members from around the world, and often has to manage expectations on both fronts. His resume reads like a global map, with leadership stints on projects spanning the UK, Finland, Sweden, the United States, Canada, Australia, India, and Bangladesh. He worked with major players like Yahoo!, Vodafone, Grameenphone, BT, and Symbian (Nokia, Ericsson, Motorola, and Panasonic), consistently earning trust across borders.

But Rasel isn't just about flashy beginnings. He was also the go to guy when a project veers off course. Whether jumping in at kickoff or mid-crisis, he brings clarity, momentum, and proven solutions often transforming projects that seemed doomed into surprising success stories. His diagnostic instincts are razor sharp: he knows how to spot the real problem and fix it before anyone else even knows it's there.

Though he prefers to be rooted in the UK, his leadership is anything but limited by geography. He has mastered the art of leading remotely bridging cultures, managing expectations, and creating genuine connections with teams in every corner of the globe. That global presence, paired with a deep respect for local nuance, makes him a rare kind of leader: equally effective in the boardrooms of London or the tech hubs of Dhaka.

If you're looking for a model of what modern, cross cultural leadership looks like in action resilient, adaptable, and relentlessly excellent, Rasel Khan's journey is one worth studying. His work is more than just management; it's a masterclass in what's possible when visionary leadership meets global complexity with heart and strategy.

Content

PART 1:

∾

NAVIGATING A GLOBAL PROFESSIONAL LANDSCAPE

THE DHAKA - TO - DUBLIN MISCOMMUNICATION

Let me tell you about a guy named Imran.

A bright, talented MBA from Dhaka University, he landed a project with a tech firm based in Ireland, his first real international gig. Everything seemed to be going great. Imran was handling the backend. The code was clean, the performance flawless. But two weeks in, the client quietly dropped him from the project.

Why?
Not because of his skills or a missed deadline - but because of an email.

The subject line he'd written read: "Here's the file."
There was no greeting, no context, and no closing line, just an attachment and a digital mic drop.

In Dhaka, this might pass as efficient. But in Dublin? It felt cold, even rude. No one had told Imran that in Western work culture, tone can matter just as much as timing. That a one line email can sink a five star performance.

That's when I realised: it's not just about knowing your stuff. It's about understanding the culture of those you are interacting with.

Welcome to the wild, wired, and wonderfully complex world of global work.

In a world more connected than ever before, the ability to thrive in international teams is no longer just nice to have - it's the key to professional success. If you're a Bangladeshi professional looking to expand your work across time zones, Slack channels, and Google Meet marathons, you're in the right place.

Here's the thing no one tells you: it's rarely your technical skills that hold you back. Most of the time, it's the *invisible stuff* - the tone of your emails, how you speak up in meetings, or how you interpret "ASAP" when your American manager sends a request on Friday at 4:30 p.m.

This book is your field guide.

It won't teach you how to be Western, because you don't need to trade your roots for results. But it will help you **bridge the gap** between the professional world you know and the unwritten rules of the Western world you want to succeed in.

I've spent more than two decades leading global teams across the UK, the US, Finland, Australia, India, and, of course, Bangladesh. I've worked with brilliant people who couldn't quite make a connection with their international colleagues, not because they weren't capable, but because no one had taught them how to understand the unspoken signals and cultural differences.

What's polite in Dhaka might come off as passive in Boston. What feels collaborative in Stockholm might feel chaotic in Chattogram.

That's where soft skills come in, those elusive, often misunderstood traits like adaptability, cultural awareness, empathy, and the fine art of knowing when (and how) to speak up.

They're the real power tools of the global workplace.

In a cross - cultural team, your technical expertise might get you through the door. But your **soft skills decide how far you'll go**, whether you'll lead meetings, manage teams, or find yourself removed from the project without ever knowing why.

Think of this book as your translator, not for language, but for meaning. It's here to help you understand cultural cues and how Western professionals think and work, as well as give you real strategies to shine without losing your identity.

We'll cover communication styles, time management, leadership dynamics, gender and inclusion challenges, and the subtle signals that shape everything from team dynamics to promotion decisions.

And don't worry - this isn't a lecture.
Each chapter comes with real world examples, relatable stories, and practical takeaways you can use right away, whether you're fresh out of university or managing a remote team across three continents.

You'll discover how to handle things like:

- When to be direct vs. diplomatic

- How to disagree without sounding disrespectful

- Why small talk matters (even if it feels awkward)

- What "work- life balance" actually means in a Western context

- How to deal with things like ableism, sexism, or just plain old office politics - in a way that keeps your dignity and your job

And while this book is written with Bangladeshi professionals in mind, the principles apply across borders. Because the truth is, empathy, adaptability, and respect don't belong to any one culture - they're universal superpowers.

So if you've ever felt confused in a team call, misread an email, or wondered why your overseas colleague seemed offended when you didn't mean anything by it - this book is for you.

By the end, you won't just be more informed - you'll be more confident, more prepared, and more at ease navigating the world of Western professionalism while staying proudly rooted in your Bengali identity.

**"Your degree gets you the job.
Your soft skills get you promoted."**
- Adapted from Peter Drucker

CHAPTER 1:
UNDERSTANDING OURSELVES

The Elevator and the Intern

A few years ago, during a project in London, I was riding the elevator with a senior Bangladeshi engineer and a young intern from Leeds. We were headed to the seventh floor for a project kickoff, and all seemed to be going smoothly.

When the elevator stopped on the third floor, the intern stepped out first and held the door open. Without looking up, the engineer walked past him, didn't say a word, and kept scrolling on his phone.

I watched the intern's face fall.

Later that day, he pulled me aside. "Is he always like that?" he asked. "I just thought . . . maybe a thank you?"

That moment stayed with me. Not because the engineer meant any harm - he didn't. Back home, it might've even been normal. But here? It came off as dismissive, entitled, even.

That's when I realized: the smallest gestures can send the loudest messages, especially when they cross cultural lines.

Before we go deeper into understanding and navigating the West, let's take a moment to look inward.

The Iceberg Model of Culture

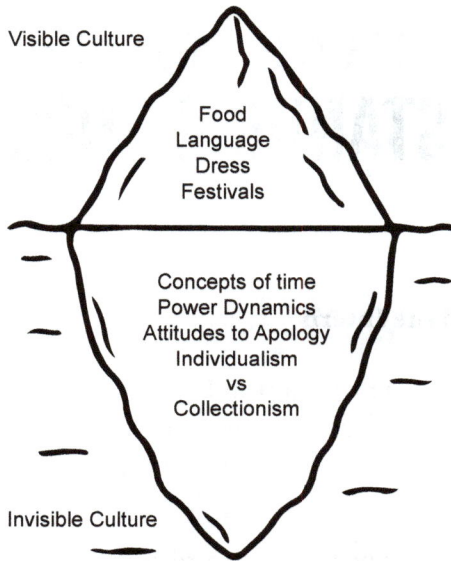

Visible Culture

Food
Language
Dress
Festivals

Concepts of time
Power Dynamics
Attitudes to Apology
Individualism
vs
Collectionism

Invisible Culture

To really understand how we're perceived in global workplaces, we need first to understand ourselves, our habits, values, and cultural defaults that seem "normal" at home but may raise eyebrows abroad. I am not criticising or blaming here, but just trying to bring awareness. Because the better we know our patterns, the more power we have to grow, adapt, and lead well.

In this chapter, we'll explore the key characteristics of Bangladeshi culture that can stand out, sometimes awkwardly, in Western professional settings. Once we see where they come from and how they're interpreted, we can start managing expectations with more intentionality.

"Culture is like an iceberg. What people see is just the tip."
–Adapted from Edward T. Hall's Iceberg Model

Entitlement: The Invisible Suitcase We Sometimes Carry

Let's start with a big one: **entitlement**.

Entitlement is not always easy to identify, but when it shows up, especially in Western settings, it tends to stick out and not in a good way.

What Is Entitlement, Really?

In our society, entitlement can be woven into everyday behavior so seamlessly that we hardly notice it. It's the unspoken idea that certain privileges, deference, or advantages are simply due to us - by rank, age, title, or social status. It becomes obvious in things like interrupting a colleague mid-sentence, expecting deference in meetings, or treating service staff dismissively.

Here's what the dictionary says:

Entitlement (noun)

1. The fact of having a right to something.

    "Full entitlement to fees and maintenance should be offered."

2. The amount to which a person has a right.

    "Her annual leave entitlement."

3. The belief that one is inherently deserving of privileges or special treatment.

    "No wonder your kids have a sense of entitlement."
    (Google 2024)

It's that third one **"inherently deserving of special treatment"** that can be problematic in Western workplaces. Cultures in the West tend to value *collaboration over hierarchy*. There's often an invisible rule: don't act like you're better than anyone. The moment someone seems entitled, they're seen as arrogant or disconnected from reality, even if that wasn't their intention.

And in many cases, it *wasn't* their intention at all.

Entitlement in Action: What It *Looks* Like on Global Teams

Here's where behavior can easily be misinterpreted: **virtual meetings**.

When someone joins a global video call and starts talking over others, dismissing ideas, or sounding like their opinion carries more weight, it might be of concern in a local context. But in a cross cultural team, those actions upset people. And often, the person doing it has no idea they've done so.

Why? Because in many Western cultures, especially in team settings, there's an unspoken expectation: **everyone's voices count, no matter what their job title is.**

Acting as if you or your opinions are more important than others' can get you labeled as "difficult," even if no one ever says it to your face.

I've seen it happen repeatedly, with both Bangladeshi professionals and others. And as someone who understands both worlds, I've often found myself wincing during meetings, watching the dynamic shift the moment someone shows even the faintest sense of superiority.

The tough part? This doesn't mean someone's a bad person. They simply don't know what they are doing and how it is being perceived. We grow up in systems that *normalize hierarchy*, even in casual settings. Whether it's how we talk to waitstaff or how we expect deference from juniors, these behaviors are part of our society, so much so that we don't even notice them.

> **"We don't see things as they are. We see them as we are."**
> *–Anaïs Nin*

So, How Do We Start Fixing It?

Watch for it in real life, in meetings, in dramas on TV. Look for the characters who expect others to wait on them or speak with unnecessary condescension. Then flip the channel. Watch a Western show or film where service staff are treated warmly and gratitude is regularly expressed. The contrast will jump out quickly.

> The first rule of soft skills:
> treat people like people, not like positions.

Scenarios to Illustrate

Let's look at a couple of scenarios to help you better understand entitlement:

Scenario 1:

A customer walks into a restaurant; loudly calls out, "Table for two;" orders without eye contact; eats quickly; throws cash on the table; and walks out without a word. Technically, he's done nothing "wrong." But the entire interaction lacked grace. He treated the staff as employees, not people. He assumed the service was owed to him.

Scenario 2:

Another customer enters; smiles; waits for the host to offer a seat; says, "Thank you"; and speaks politely throughout. He thanks the waiter for the meal, pays, and says goodbye. Again, nothing fancy. But the human element is present.

To someone raised in Scenario 1 culture, Scenario 2 may seem overly nice or even unnecessary. But in the West, Scenario 2 is expected. Scenario 1 comes across as entitled.

If you carry a, "I paid, so I don't need to be polite," mindset into professional spaces, especially international ones, it won't go unnoticed. And it won't help you grow.

Here's the key: start noticing.

Who thanks whom? Who interrupts whom? Who expects what from whom?

If you start from the belief that no one owes you anything, not the waiter, not your assistant, not your teammate halfway across the globe, you begin to show up differently. Gratitude naturally follows. And with it, respect.

Try This:

- Ask a friend or colleague to observe your behavior for a week. Invite them to gently note the moments you might come off as entitled, especially in group settings.

- Start a "gratitude audit." Each day, list who helped you and whether you thanked them. Even small moments count.

In my workshops on this topic, the pattern is always the same. At first, participants identify the *obvious* signs of entitlement. Then, as we dig deeper, more subtle layers emerge hierarchical speech patterns, expectations of deference, and unconscious status displays.

Once you see it, you can't unsee it.
And that's the beginning of transformation.

Cultural Blind Spot: Entitlement
In Western workplaces, entitlement often signals arrogance - not confidence. Expecting special treatment without earning it can make you seem rude. Self-awareness is the first step to shifting the perception.

Hero Syndrome: When Good Intentions Go Rogue

Now let's talk about something many of us know all too well: the need to be a hero.

This is the urge to swoop in, fix everything, and earn the spotlight. It's that inner voice that says, "If I don't save this project, who will?"

In high pressure environments, especially across the Indian subcontinent, that kind of self-driven hustle is celebrated. It's how many of us were raised, to prove ourselves through action, speed, and solutions.

But in a global team? That solo savior energy is not always translated the same way.

It can make others feel left out. Or worse, unneeded.
And if it becomes a habit, it risks undermining team cohesion. People might stop collaborating and instead just wait for the "hero" to save the day.

That's not leadership. That's burnout waiting to happen.

> **"If you want to go fast, go alone.**
> **If you want to go far, go together."**
> *-African Proverb*Now, here's the good news: heroism can evolve.

As we mature, both personally and professionally, that need to be "the one" tends to shift. Instead of rescuing others, we learn to **equip** them. Instead of seeking credit, we spread it around.

Real leadership doesn't come from solo acts, it comes from building teams that are strong enough not to need heroes.

That doesn't mean we stop stepping up.
It means we learn to step aside sometimes, too.

So if you've ever felt that urge to take it all on, to fix everything yourself, pause and ask yourself:

- Am I lifting the team?

- Or am I quietly undermining them?

True heroism in the global workplace is humble, consistent, and shared.

Generosity: Our Superpower (When Framed Right)

If you've ever been invited into a Bangladeshi home, you know about the insistence on food, and second helpings, how your plate is refilled before you even say yes.

Generosity is just part of our culture, and it is one of our most beautiful traits. It shows up in our communities, our families, and even in the workplace. Whether it's offering to help a colleague with their report, covering for a teammate, or bringing sweets for the office after Eid - it's second nature.

But here's where things get complicated: **generosity without context can be misread**.

In Western settings, especially in corporate environments where boundaries rule, generosity can be seen as a way to win favor or manipulate others in some way.

Why is he offering to do that extra work?
Is she trying to win favors?
Are they expecting something in return?

That's not what we meant, of course. But unless we're clear about our *why*, our well meaning actions can raise eyebrows.

Tip:

Generosity + Transparency = Trust.
Be generous, but explain your intention. "Hey, I have some extra time. Can I help with something?" is a small phrase that goes a long way.

The fix isn't to stop being generous, it's to help others understand why you are doing it. When colleagues know that our generosity comes from values, not to get something in return, it strengthens relationships instead of shuts them down.

And if we can help our Western peers understand the heart behind it, we don't just avoid confusion, we showcase one of the strongest parts of our cultural DNA.

Takeaways

Self-awareness isn't about self-judgment. It's about noticing what we do, and then choosing how we want to show up.

From entitlement to empathy, from thankless habits to generous leadership, we have *incredible* cultural strengths. We just need to learn how to frame them so they translate across cultures.

When we understand ourselves clearly, as well as the culture we are relating to, we show up more effectively.

CHAPTER 2:
WESTERN PROFESSIONAL NORMS

The "Hi, Mike" Email Disaster

Rafiq had just landed a dream contract with a mid sized tech firm based in Chicago. Eager to impress, he dove right in, joining meetings, writing up reports, delivering on every milestone.

Then came the first email to the CEO.

Subject line: "Project Timeline."
Opening line: "Respected Sir, I hope this message finds you in good health and high spirits . . ."

That's when the red flags went up.

The CEO, Mike, who introduced himself as "just Mike" in their first meeting - forwarded the email to the HR manager with a note: "Is this sarcasm?"

It wasn't sarcasm. It was just cultural.

Rafiq didn't know that in the American workplace, calling someone "Respected Sir" can feel weirdly formal - almost like you're being passive-aggressive. He meant it as a sign of respect, but Mike read it as sarcasm or distance.

And just like that, a small cultural misunderstanding began to overshadow an otherwise excellent performance.

Welcome to Western workplace culture, where the rules are real, but no one gives you the manual.

What Makes Western Work Culture . . . Western?

In today's fast paced, hyper connected world, knowing how to write good code or run a great campaign isn't enough. If you're working across borders - especially in Western contexts - you also need to know how people work, communicate, and think.

And spoiler alert: it's not always what we're used to.

For Bangladeshi professionals stepping into teams with colleagues from the US, UK, or Europe, there can be a sharp contrast in expectations, style, and etiquette. What might feel polite and proper in Dhaka could come off as stiff or indirect in Dallas.

The good news? These differences are learnable. And once you see them clearly, they stop being obstacles and start becoming tools.

Direct Communication: Say What You Mean (Really)

Let's start with one of the biggest shifts: clarity and directness.

The two paths of feedback

Bengali Context	Western Context
lirect Communication	Direct Communication

Bengali Context (lirect Communication):
- Manager / Peer
- Harmony
- Saving Face
- Subtlety
- Recipient

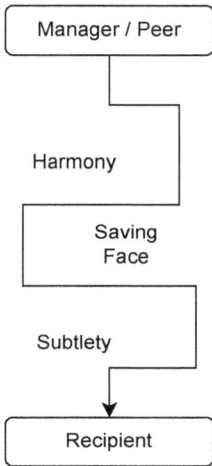

Western Context (Direct Communication):
- Manager / Peer
- Clarity
- Focus on the issue not the person
- Goal Orientated
- Recipient

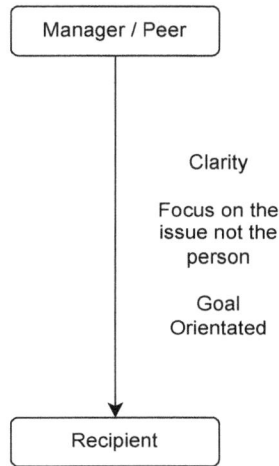

In most Western professional settings especially in North America and Northern Europe **direct communication** is the gold standard. Team members are expected to speak up, voice opinions, ask questions, and give feedback openly.

This isn't seen as confrontational. It's seen as collaborative.

Being too subtle can sometimes work against you. In fact, not saying what you think might lead colleagues to believe you either:

- Don't understand the topic,
- Don't care about the outcome,
- Or are being passive-aggressive.

None of those are great options.

The idea behind directness isn't to be harsh. It's to be transparent to help everyone stay aligned, fix issues early, and move forward quickly. The sooner everyone knows the truth, the faster the team can act.

Side Note: But What About the British?

Ah, the Brits. Just when you've got the hang of saying things directly, here comes the curveball: **sarcasm**.

The British (and to some extent, Canadians and Australians) love a bit of dry humor and subtle irony. "With all due respect . . ." doesn't always mean respect is coming. And if someone says, "Interesting idea," there's a good chance they mean the opposite.

We'll dive into this cultural puzzle more in a later chapter. For now, just know: **context matters**.

Individualism + Team Spirit = The Western Work Equation

In Western cultures, especially in the US, individual achievement is highly valued. Promotions often go to those who "own" their work, speak up in meetings, and take initiative without waiting for instruction.

But that doesn't mean teamwork takes a back seat.

In fact, the best professionals are expected to balance both:

- **Take personal responsibility**, and

- **Help the team win**.

That's the sweet spot.

The phrase *"collaborate without being a pushover"* is basically an unspoken mantra in many companies. You're not just responsible for your task - you're expected to support the group's success.

Work – Life Balance: A Modern Western Value

If your manager logs off at 5:00 p.m. sharp and doesn't reply to your email until the next day, don't panic. You probably didn't offend them - they're just protecting their **work life balance**.

Unlike in some Asian contexts where long hours are often worn as a badge of honor, Western workplaces are increasingly embracing the idea that **rest makes you better**. Flexible hours, remote work, and even four day workweeks are gaining popularity.

It doesn't mean people don't care. It means they believe in **sustainable performance** and that boundaries are a form of professionalism, not laziness.

First Names, Big Ideas: The Culture of Informality

In a US or UK office, you'll often see interns addressing CEOs by their **first name**.

At first, this might feel jarring especially if you come from a culture where titles like "sir," "madam," or "manager" are standard. But in the West, **informality is not a lack of respect**. It's a signal of openness, accessibility, and trust.

It's not unusual for a twenty three year old software engineer to pitch a bold idea to a fifty five year old director - and be taken seriously. That's the point.

This flattening of hierarchy is intentional. It creates space for innovation, fast decision - making, and genuine collaboration. In creative and tech industries especially, formality can even be a barrier.

Managers Who Actually Listen

In many Western companies, managers are judged not just by what *they* accomplish but by how well they **bring out the best in their teams**.

That's why many workplaces encourage open door policies, regular check ins, and feedback sessions - to keep communication clear and ongoing. A good manager doesn't need all the answers - just the wisdom to let others shine.

First Names & Flat Hierarchies

In the UK and US, calling your manager - or even the CEO - by their first name isn't considered disrespectful. It's actually normal. This casual tone reflects a "flatter" workplace culture, where titles take a back seat to open dialogue and shared ideas. The goal? To make sure everyone feels comfortable speaking up, no matter their job title.

Participatory Decision - Making: Everyone Gets a Vote

In Western workplaces, the boss doesn't always make the final decision on everything, not alone, anyway.

In many organizations, especially in the US and UK, **decision - making is a team sport**. It's participatory and inclusive, and everyone gets a vote. The idea? If a decision affects everyone, then everyone should have a chance to shape it.

This isn't just a feel good concept. It's strategy.

When leaders invite input from all levels of the company, from interns to executives, they aren't just being nice, they're being smart. Different perspectives bring different solutions, and more often than not, better ones.

Take this real world example:

At an American manufacturing company, senior leaders don't just hand down top down memos about how the line should run. Instead, they hold regular cross - functional meetings. People from across the org chart factory workers, supervisors, engineers, and VPs - come together to improve production. Everyone in the room has a stake in the outcome, so everyone gets a say.

This approach not only creates better processes, but it also builds buy in. People are more invested in outcomes they helped create.

So what's the manager's role in all of this?

They facilitate.
Not dictate.
They guide conversations, encourage quieter voices, and help steer the team toward decisions that balance creativity, feasibility, and fairness.

That shift - from, "I'm the boss, do as I say," to, "I'm the guide, what do you think?"- is one of the defining features of modern Western leadership. And it's changing the way teams operate.

When companies embrace participatory decision making, three things happen:

1. **Innovation goes up.** More ideas on the table mean more potential breakthroughs.

2. **Trust grows.** People feel seen, heard, and respected.

3. **Adaptability increases.** Diverse perspectives help teams respond faster and smarter to change.

This kind of leadership also aligns with the cultural value of **fairness**. In Western contexts, fairness isn't just about equal outcomes - it's about *equal voice*. People want to know that decisions are made thoughtfully, not randomly or behind closed doors. And when transparency is part of the process, it builds confidence across the entire organization.

You don't have to be the CEO to experience this. You might see it in the way a team leader runs a project kickoff, a product manager collects user feedback, or a company handles internal changes, by inviting input, not imposing solutions.

In short:
Participation isn't just welcome, it's expected.

Participatory Systems

In Western workplaces, participation isn't a buzzword, it's baked into the system.

Companies don't just *say* they want your input. They build structures that make it possible. You will find formal committees, advisory councils, peer review panels and even informal "feedback lunches," where employees sit down with senior leadership and offer suggestions face-to-face.

You'll also see "open door policies" in action, sometimes literally. In one UK company I visited, the director's office didn't even have a door, just a glass panel and a round table. The message was clear: if you've got something to say, come in and say it.

This accessibility isn't accidental. It reflects a deep cultural value: **fairness through transparency**.

When people at every level of the organization are invited to weigh in, the outcome is more than just a better decision, it's a **stronger, more motivated team**. People feel trusted and heard, and that changes how they work.

Western workplaces see this not only as good leadership but as a **strategic edge**. In fast moving industries, the best ideas often come from unexpected places. And participatory systems make sure those ideas rise to the surface.

Learning from the Past, Growing into the Future

There's something else Western organizations do particularly well: they **pay attention to history,** especially their own.

The culture of continuous improvement is more than a management fad. It's a mindset. And it shows up in three key ways:

1. **Feedback**

2. **Reflection**

3. **Growth**

Let's break those down.

Feedback That Actually Helps

In many Western companies, feedback isn't something you get once a year in a stuffy HR meeting. It's ongoing, expected, and even welcomed.

Take, for example, a US based consulting firm I worked with. Every quarter, employees sit down for detailed reviews, not just with their managers, but with peers as well. These sessions highlight both achievements and areas for development, usually ending with a clear, actionable plan.

And here's the twist: it's not about pointing fingers.
It's about **building people up**.

When feedback is handled constructively, it doesn't feel like criticism. It feels like investment.

This kind of culture creates an environment where employees can be vulnerable without fear, knowing the goal is growth, not punishment. Managers become mentors. Colleagues become coaches. And teams become stronger.

Training, Mentorship, and the Growth Mindset

Continuous improvement doesn't stop at feedback. Western organizations are big believers in **professional development** training programs, mentorship, online courses, even sabbaticals for deep learning.

The belief is simple: **develop your people, and the organization grows with them**.

And it works.

In these workplaces, mistakes aren't failures, they're part of how you learn, grow, and get better. This mindset creates resilience, adaptability, and a team that's better equipped to handle change, pressure, and complexity.

In a fast changing global economy, that kind of mindset isn't just helpful, it's essential.

Next, let's talk about something that is important to Westerners but may not always be as straightforward as some of the other concepts: time management.

Time Management

Let's set the scene: you show up to a 10:00 a.m. meeting at 10:07, heart racing, shirt slightly damp from the humidity, and you smile politely. But instead of a warm welcome, you're met with awkward silence and a few glances at the clock.

You think: "Seven minutes isn't that late."

They think: "This person can't be trusted."

Welcome to one of the sharpest cultural disconnects in global professionalism, **how we treat time.**

In Bangladesh, time is fluid, social, and forgiving. In many Western workplaces, time is a contract, measured, monitored, and strictly enforced. It's not just about being punctual. It's about being seen as reliable, prepared, and professional.

So if you're wondering why being a few minutes late caused such a chill in the room, or why "just rescheduling" made your manager visibly twitch, you're not alone. Time, in the Western professional world, isn't just a schedule. It's a statement.

Let's break it down. And more importantly, let's learn how to manage time without losing your soul.

Bangladeshi Time: Elastic, Fluid, and Mysteriously Nonlinear

In Bangladesh, "I'll be there in ten minutes" could mean *ten* actual minutes . . . or it could mean after tea, traffic, and a phone call with your cousin in Sylhet. Time flows differently here. It bends, stretches, and adapts to the moment.

This isn't due to laziness or disrespect, it's deeply rooted in a communal lifestyle. Personal connections often take precedence over clock precision. You might be late because your neighbor needed help, or because your rickshaw driver stopped for a quick snack. The mindset is relational, not transactional. Being flexible is part of being human.

But that same flexibility can come across very differently in Western settings.

Western Time: Sharp, Structured, and Relentlessly Punctual

In Western cultures, especially the UK, Germany, or Switzerland punctuality is practically sacred. Being late doesn't just inconvenience someone. It implies you don't value their time. It suggests a lack of planning, discipline, or even professionalism.

And there's often an unspoken assumption: "If you can't be on time, how can I trust you with anything else?"

Harsh? Maybe. But that's the framework.

Of course, it helps that transportation systems run more reliably and that schedules are often built around individual efficiency. Still, the expectation is clear: if you say 10:00 a.m., you don't stroll in at 10:17 smiling and saying, "Traffic."

Bridging the Gap: Time Management Without Losing Your Mind (or Your Friends)

So, how do you, a global Bengali navigating both systems, honor your roots *and* respect Western professionalism?

You get smart about time.

1. **Awareness is Your Superpower**

Understand the cultural expectations wherever you are. If you're meeting someone from a time sensitive culture, show up early. If you're working with someone more flexible, allow breathing room, but still communicate clearly.

2. **Build in Buffers**

Leave earlier than you think you need to. Add padding to your calendar. That thirty minute drive? Plan for forty five. That way, if a monsoon shows up or your Uber driver decides to circle the block four times, you're still on time.

3. **Communicate Like a Pro**

Running late? Don't just leave them wondering where you are or if you will show up. Send a quick message. Acknowledge the delay. Offer a new estimated time. It shows respect and builds trust, even though you are late.

4. **Use the Tools of the Trade**

Set reminders. Use calendar apps. Share invites. Send confirmations. These small actions help bridge the cultural divide between casual and structured.

Time Isn't the Enemy, Disrespect Is

At the heart of it, good time management isn't about being robotic. It's about showing respect. It's saying, "I see you. I value your time. I'm here because I said I would be."

You don't have to abandon your cultural roots to be professional. You just need to be aware of cultural expectations and plan accordingly.

Time is a Sign of Respect
Being on time shows respect. Being consistently late shows your priorities are somewhere else.

Bringing It All Together

Western workplace culture comes with many things that may not feel natural at first, including getting direct feedback, being on a first name basis with your boss, and having constant evaluations. But if you understand the reasoning behind these practices, they start to make sense.

- Participation isn't just nice - it's how good ideas happen.

- Feedback isn't a threat - it's a guide.

- Mistakes aren't failures - they give you a plan for the future.

- Time management equals respect for other's time.

And for professionals transitioning from Southeast Asian workplaces to Western ones, understanding this culture is key. At first, the informality, the expectation of autonomy, and the emphasis on work life boundaries might feel uncomfortable.

But over time, many come to appreciate how empowering it can be.

Once you understand the *why* behind the *what*, you'll start to navigate these new settings with more confidence. You'll stop second guessing every email and start contributing in ways that feel natural for you, and are effective.

In the end, Western work culture isn't about abandoning your identity, it's about learning new tools to succeed.

PART 2

MASTERING PROFESSIONAL COMMUNICATION AND ETIQUETTE

CHAPTER 3:
COMMUNICATING TO CONNECT

The Power of One Word

When Shoma started her new job in Toronto, she brought with her everything she thought mattered technical expertise, a strong work ethic, and perfect grammar.

What she didn't bring? A habit of saying "please."

She wasn't rude. Just efficient. In Dhaka, politeness was wrapped in tone and body language, not stuffed into every sentence.

But after a few weeks, her manager gently pulled her aside.

"Your emails are clear," he said, "but they feel abrupt."

That puzzled her. She reread one:

"Send me the updated report by 3 p.m."

Technically correct. Perfect grammar. No insults in sight.

But then she noticed how her Canadian colleagues wrote:

"Could you please send me the updated report by 3 p.m.? Thanks!"

Same request. Different tone. Warmer. Less like a command, more like a collaboration.

It wasn't about begging or losing authority. It was about softening the edges. Inviting cooperation. Building rapport.

So Shoma added one word - *please* - and watched her relationships shift. People smiled more and replied faster. Meetings got easier.

Sometimes, in cross cultural communication, it's not what you say, it's how you say it.

When you step into a global professional space, your technical skills get you noticed. But it's your **social instincts**, the way you communicate, apologize, show gratitude, handle tension - that determine whether you build trust or create confusion. We'll walk you through the important things to know in this chapter.

The Invisible Rules of Interaction

In chapter 1 we talked a little about knowing ourselves and how some of our habits, rooted in our culture, are different from those in Western societies. This chapter will go deeper into those social instincts, the invisible rules of interaction that can make or break relationships across cultures to help us be more effective in dealing with our Western counterparts.

We'll explore nonverbal communication, expressions like "Thank you" and "Sorry" more deeply, so you can understand when to use them and the different things they can mean, which vary drastically from the meaning they carry to us in our culture. Understanding these differences will go a long way toward creating better relationships with Westerners.

Body Language, Personal Space, and Boundaries

The Accidental Offense – Western Edition

Rashid had only been in Toronto a week when he met his new manager at a company happy hour. Eager to make a good impression, he leaned in warmly, shook both her hands, and asked if she had eaten, because, of course, that's what you ask someone you respect. She blinked, took a tiny step back, and smiled politely. The conversation ended quickly.

Later, a colleague pulled him aside and gently explained: "Hey, just so you know, in Canada, people usually prefer a bit more personal space- and asking about food in that context can feel a little odd."

Rashid wasn't being rude. He was being Bengali.

But in that moment, he'd unknowingly crossed a few unspoken Western boundaries: personal space, small talk etiquette, and physical formality.

In Bangladesh, warmth often means **closeness** - checking in with people about meals, leaning in while speaking, maybe even a friendly tap on the shoulder. But in many Western settings, that same behaviour can be seen as **too familiar, too soon**. People may interpret it as pushy, flirtatious, or just socially awkward.

In Western workplaces:

- **Eye contact** shows confidence (but don't turn it into a staring contest).

- **Handshakes** are firm, quick, and usually involve just one hand.

- **Physical space** is sacred - stand too close, and people may literally back away.

- **Touching** (even friendly pats) is reserved for close relationships, not colleagues you just met.

- **"How are you?"** doesn't mean "Tell me your problems." It usually just means "Hello."

So what should a Bangladeshi professional do?

Observe first.
Before jumping into a conversation, take a moment to see how others are interacting. How far apart are they standing? Are they smiling or staying neutral? Are they touching, gesturing, nodding?**Mirror modestly.**

No need to fake it - but gently mirroring the social tone shows awareness and respect. You're not abandoning your roots, you're learning the "accent" of the culture you're in.

When unsure, ask.
It's okay to say, "Hey, I'm still getting used to how things work here - should I be doing anything differently?" Most people appreciate honesty and cultural curiosity.

Remember: In the West, **boundaries are not a rejection**. They're a default setting. Respecting them doesn't mean distancing yourself from others. It simply creates a foundation of trust, one that, over time, opens doors to genuine connection.

The Power of "Thank You" and "Sorry": Small Words, Big Signals

I can't count how many times a Bengali friend has looked at me, amused or baffled, and said something like:

"You say 'thank you' *so much*. Are you trying to win an award?"

Fair question. And to them, it probably did look excessive. But to someone raised in Western culture, especially in the UK, those two little words are what society runs on.

Let's break it down.

In Western cultures, particularly in Britain, "thank you" is expected - not just for grand favours but for the smallest interactions:

Handing over a receipt? Thank you.

Holding the door? Thank you.

Answering a question in a meeting? Definitely, thank you.

It's not about flattery. It's about respect and not taking people, or their efforts, for granted. Even when someone is doing their job, the default assumption is: "Acknowledge them. Always."

The same goes for "sorry." It's not necessarily an admission of guilt. Sometimes, it's just a way to keep social gears running smoothly:

"Sorry, could you repeat that?"

"Sorry, I didn't catch your name."

"Sorry to interrupt . . ."

It's a sign of consideration, a way to say, "I see you, and I respect your space."

Now, contrast that with Bangladeshi culture, where these same words don't always carry the same weight, or show up as often.

In Bangladesh, gratitude is often shown through actions. If someone helps you, you don't always say thank you - you *do* something for them later. You return the favor. You check in. You show loyalty over time.

Saying "thank you" out loud can sometimes feel awkward or overly formal. Why speak what can be shown? After all, if the relationship is strong, shouldn't it be understood?

Similarly, apologies can feel heavy - like true admissions of fault. Saying sorry might imply wrongdoing or weakness, so many people avoid using it unless they feel genuinely responsible.

These aren't wrong approaches. They're just different cultural interpretations of respect and sincerity.

But here's the challenge: when you're navigating a Western workplace, that difference can lead to misunderstandings.

To a Western colleague, the absence of "Thank you" might feel dismissive.

To a Bengali professional, the constant apologies might feel unnecessary, or even disingenuous.

Two Cultures, One Goal: Respect

What matters most isn't *which* method you use - it's whether the other person **understands your intention**.

That's why cultural flexibility matters.

If you're working in the West, learn to say "thank you" and "sorry" more freely. It won't make you look weak - it'll make you relatable.

The Significance of Apologies: Empathy Over Admission

Let's say you're walking down a crowded hallway and you accidentally bump someone's shoulder.

If you're in London, you both immediately say, "Sorry"- even if they're the one who ran into you.

If you're in Dhaka, things might play out differently. The response might be a raised eyebrow, a head tilt, maybe a subtle repositioning. But a verbal "sorry"? Probably not.

This isn't about one culture being polite and another being rude. It's about how we interpret apologies, what they mean, when they're appropriate, and what they cost.

In power centric cultures like Bangladesh, status and authority are often tightly interwoven. In those settings, apologising isn't always seen as a gracious act - it can feel like an admission of weakness. Saying "sorry" might imply fault, and fault can be a threat to one's standing.

So, many people hold back. They let moments pass without acknowledgement, or offer apologies only in moments of deep misfortune - like the loss of a loved one or a tragedy affecting someone's life. Even then, apologies may sound hesitant or, paradoxically, overly emotional because the moment has grown too large for words alone.

The result? A cultural tendency to treat apologies as something heavy, something used sparingly, and only when absolutely necessary.

But in **many Western cultures**, especially in the UK, apologies aren't about guilt. They're about **empathy**.

Saying "sorry" isn't necessarily a confession. It's an acknowledgement. It tells the other person, "I see that you were affected, and I care."

That simple gesture, often overlooked, goes a long way toward building mutual respect.

Here are a few classic Western apology moments:

For accidental impact:
You bump into someone in a café queue. "Sorry!" is immediate. Whether it was your fault or not doesn't matter. What matters is **recognising the impact**.

To express sympathy:
Your colleague just lost a family member. You say, "I'm so sorry for your loss." No one thinks you caused it, and you're not admitting guilt. You're expressing solidarity and compassion.

To acknowledge disruption:
Say you're about to interrupt a meeting to clarify something. You should say, "Sorry to interrupt, but I just want to ask . . ." Again, this is not guilt, just a subtle social cue that says, "I value your time, and I know I'm stepping in."

In all of these examples, apologies are used to bring people together and let them know you care and they matter. They're not dramatic confessions, they're signs of thoughtfulness.

The big takeaway: In global teams, understanding how different cultures use (or don't use) apologies can **make or break trust**.

If you're working with Western colleagues and rarely say "sorry," they may perceive you as indifferent, arrogant, or dismissive, even if that couldn't be further from the truth.

What Makes an Apology Effective?

A real apology has one job: **to acknowledge the other person's experience**.

That's it.

It doesn't need to explain your side. It doesn't need to justify your behaviour. In fact, offering too much explanation can weaken the message. A genuine apology stands on its own.

"I'm really sorry for the inconvenience."

"I didn't realise that caused so much trouble. I apologise."

"Sorry about that. I'll make sure it doesn't happen again."

Simple. Direct. Human.

So, the next time someone comments on how often you say "thank you" or "sorry," take it as a compliment. You're showing up with empathy. And in today's global workplace, that's not just appreciated, it's essential.

The Anatomy of a Real Apology
A real apology isn't a defense - it's an acknowledgment. In professional settings, that means focusing on the impact your actions had, not justifying why they happened. Intent matters, but impact speaks louder.

Cultivating the Habit: A Practical Path to Fluency

If saying "thank you" or "sorry" doesn't come naturally to you yet, don't worry, you're not alone.

For many professionals transitioning into the Western workplace culture, these tiny phrases can feel awkward at first. Forced. Even performative. You might find yourself thinking, "Why should I say sorry for something that wasn't my fault?" or "Do I really need to thank someone for doing their job?"

Here's the truth: cultural fluency is just like any other skill, it's **trainable**.

And the good news? You don't need flashcards or formal coaching. You just need to pay attention.

Try this as an experiment. For one full day, make a conscious effort to notice moments that deserve gratitude or might benefit from a brief apology. Don't overthink it, just look for opportunities to express those small social signals.

Set a goal of saying **30 "Thank you"s and 30 "Sorrys"**.

Sound like a lot? It's not. Once you tune in, you'll realize these moments are everywhere.

Examples of "Thank You" Moments:

- Someone made you breakfast. Even if it was toast, you didn't make it.

- The bus driver got you to work safely. Thank them.

- You slept in a bed last night. Yes, that counts. Gratitude isn't just for other people - it's for life.

- A colleague made you a cup of tea - even if you paid for it. Thank them anyway. It wasn't just tea - it was care.

Examples of "Sorry" Moments:

- You said something that landed wrong - even though you meant well.

- You accidentally interrupted someone mid-sentence.

- You had to ask someone to move so you could pass. That's a small disruption. Say sorry.

At first, this will feel mechanical. You'll wonder if you're overdoing it. Then something strange will happen: You'll begin to **feel** the moments before they happen. Your instincts will sharpen. And you'll start noticing when other people don't say thank you . . . or when no one apologises for something they should have.

That awareness? That's the final step.

At that point, you are no longer acting out a script, but have acquired a new level of communication, one that works well with your Western counterparts.

This is how cultural habits are formed: not through theory, but through practice.

And the more fluent you become in these micro moments, the more natural they'll feel - and the more they'll open doors, smooth interactions, and build trust wherever you go.

The Power of "Sorry" & "Thank You"
In Western workplaces, "sorry" shows empathy, not guilt. "Thank you" shows respect - not weakness. Using both sincerely builds trust and keeps relationships strong.

The Power of "Please"

Again, it is just one word, but "please" has the power to change how we're perceived in nearly every social and professional interaction with Westerners.

And yet, despite its simplicity, "please" is one of the most **culturally misunderstood** words in the global lexicon.

Let's unpack it.

In the West: "Please" as a Social Lubricant

In Western cultures, especially the UK and US, "please" isn't optional. It's part of the unspoken script of polite society.

When someone says, "Can you email me the file?" it might sound abrupt. But, "Could you please email me the file?" is a different story.

It softens the tone, signals respect, and leaves room for the other person to say no (even if they won't).

That's the beauty of "please" in the West: it's not just about manners, it's about **mutual respect**. You're not barking orders. You're offering a choice-an invitation to collaborate, not comply.

In many workplaces, particularly in English - speaking nations, forgetting "please" can be seen as cold or demanding, even if your tone is neutral. It's a small word with big social impact.

How to Use "Please" Appropriately

Here are some clear and culturally appropriate examples of using "please" in a Western professional setting:

Formal Requests (Email or Written Communication)

- "Could you please review the attached document by Friday?"

- "Please let me know if you need any clarification."

- "Would you please confirm your availability for the meeting?"

Team Collaboration (Meetings or Messages)

- "Please share your thoughts when you get a chance."

- "Can you please add that to the agenda?"

- "Let's please keep comments brief so everyone has time to speak."

Casual Verbal Use (Still Polite)

- "Pass me the file, please."

- "Please hold on - I'll check that for you."

- "Hey, can you please help me with this for a second?"

Even When Delegating as a Manager

- "Please follow up with the client this afternoon."

- "Let's please make sure this goes out before noon."

- "Could you please take the lead on this part of the project?"

In short, use "please" to soften instructions, show professionalism, and maintain respect - especially in writing and formal settings.

Humor and Sarcasm

Humor is a wonderful thing. It can dissolve tension in a room, pull a team together, and turn a boring Monday into something halfway bearable. In Western workplaces especially, humor isn't just entertainment, it's part of building relationships. It helps people connect, relax, and feel human in the midst of deadlines and PowerPoints.

But here's the key: humor is very cultural.

What people find funny in Boston may not be funny or may even confuse or offend people in Dhaka, Delhi, or Seoul. And it's not because one culture is funnier than another. It's because humor is deeply cultural. The jokes, references, tone, timing, and even body language can vary wildly.

So let's explore the dos and don'ts of navigating humor in the West, and what to do when you have *no idea* why everyone is laughing.

Banter, Idioms, and Insider Signals

In many English speaking countries, "banter" is practically a language of its own. It's light teasing, witty comebacks, and playful sarcasm all rolled into one. Banter is a way to say, "I like you," without actually saying it. If someone teases you at work, it's often a sign that you've been accepted into the inner circle.

Then there are the idioms:
"Kick the bucket."
"Bite the bullet."
"Throw someone under the bus."

These phrases sound strange if you take them literally, and totally confusing if you've never heard them before. But understanding them signals cultural fluency. When you get the joke, or at least the reference, it shows you're part of the group.

If you don't get it? Don't fake it. Just ask.

Saying, "I haven't heard that one before - what does it mean?" almost always leads to an explanation, a laugh, and a stronger connection. People love explaining their favorite references. It makes them feel seen. And by asking, you walk away knowing one more thing than you did five minutes ago.

Sarcasm: Not Always Just a Joke

Let's talk about sarcasm.

In many Western settings, sarcasm is more than humor, it's a subtle, socially acceptable way of expressing frustration. It helps people vent without getting overtly confrontational.

For instance, if a colleague says, "Well, that went perfectly," after a meeting that clearly didn't, they're probably not celebrating. They're expressing disappointment, with a side of humor.

For someone unfamiliar with this tone, it's easy to misread sarcasm as a joke. You might laugh along, thinking you're building rapport, while your colleague is actually fuming inside. (Don't worry - it happens to the best of us.)

The key? Tune in to context, tone, and facial expressions. And when in doubt, ask: "Just checking - are you serious or being sarcastic?"

It's a fair question. And it shows you care enough to listen closely.

Pop Culture Punchlines: When Everyone's Quoting Movies

Another layer of Western humor is built on popular culture - especially movies and TV shows. If you've spent time in the UK or US workplace, you've probably heard someone say something like:

- "May the Force be with you." (*Star Wars*)

- "I'm gonna make him an offer he can't refuse." (*The Godfather*)

- "Life moves pretty fast. If you don't stop and look around once in a while, you could miss it." (*Ferris Bueller's Day Off*)

These quotes are everywhere, sprinkled into meetings, emails, even casual coffee chats. And sometimes, the joke hinges on you knowing exactly where the quote came from and what it implies.

So what if you don't?

You say: "Oh, I haven't heard that one - what's it from?"

Most people light up when asked. They'll tell you the reference, the backstory, and maybe even recommend the movie (likely followed by, "Wait, you've never seen that?!"). Suddenly, you've gone from outsider to someone people enjoy talking to.

Here are just a few of the big hitters you might hear in a Western office:

From *Star Trek*

- "To boldly go where no man has gone before."

- "Resistance is futile."

- "It's life, Jim, but not as we know it."

From *Star Wars*

- "May the Force be with you."

From *The Godfather*

- "I'm gonna make him an offer he can't refuse."

- "It's not personal, it's strictly business."

- "Keep your friends close, but your enemies closer."

- "Leave the gun. Take the cannoli."

From *Ferris Bueller's Day Off*

- "Life moves pretty fast . . ."

- "Bueller? . . . Bueller?"

- "What *aren't* we going to do?"

Bonus references often pop up from *Top Gun*, *Dirty Dancing*, and *Pulp Fiction*. You don't need to know them all - but recognizing them can help you feel more in sync with workplace culture. The popular legal drama 'Suits' frequently shows protagonists using movie references.

And if not? Asking about them can build bridges even faster than pretending you know.

The bottom line is this: Humor is a fantastic connector, but it's also a potential minefield if misunderstood. Lean into curiosity. Ask questions. Be open. And remember: you don't need to be the funniest person in the room to earn respect, you just need to be real.

Decoding Sarcasm and Humor

If someone makes a joke or says something you don't quite understand, just ask. Most people enjoy explaining - it builds connection. But be aware: in many Western settings, sarcasm isn't always just for laughs. Sometimes, it hides annoyance or criticism. Pay attention to tone and body language to read the situation more clearly.

Conclusion: Communication That Connects

The best communicators aren't the ones who talk the most, they're the ones who know how to build bridges. When you learn to listen deeply, observe thoughtfully, and speak with both clarity and empathy, you step into a new level of professional influence. Whether it's reading between the lines of an email or navigating an awkward silence in a meeting, your ability to understand and adapt across cultures will set you apart.

Communication that connects is a skill you build and a gift you give. It's how trust grows, how teams thrive, and how you rise, not just as a professional, but as a respected voice in any room you enter.

CHAPTER 4:
CONFLICT, CRITICISM, AND APOLOGIES

The Angry Uncle and the Silent Office

Back in Dhaka, Sumon's uncle ran a textile business like a general leading an army. He shouted from the stairs, slammed files on desks, and barked instructions that echoed through the hallways. No one took it personally. It was just how he showed urgency, passion, leadership.

Sumon grew up thinking this was normal, that raising your voice was just part of being in charge.

Then he moved to Toronto.

At his first team meeting, he got frustrated when a junior developer missed a key deadline. Without thinking, he raised his voice, not a yell, just a sharp tone, a pointed question. The room went quiet and heads turned. His manager's smile froze mid expression.

Later that day, HR asked to "check in."

That's when Sumon learned: in many Western workplaces, loud emotions, even if well meaning raise red flags. What felt like energy and involvement in Bangladesh came off as aggression in Canada.

He hadn't meant to intimidate anyone. But in this new environment, the volume of his voice could be louder than the content of his words.

It took time, reflection, and a few awkward moments, but Sumon eventually learned how to dial back the volume without losing his voice. And when a teammate apologized to him one day for a minor mistake, he finally understood Western professionalism isn't emotionless, but it expresses emotion differently.

In this chapter, we will walk through how to better express anger in a Western setting, show you a few ways to handle disagreements, listen better, and communicate more effectively with your Western counterparts.

Anger

Let's talk about anger, the red hot, fist clenching, chest tightening emotion we've all felt but rarely discuss in professional settings.

Anger may be universal, but how it shows up is anything but.

In Bangladesh, for example, you might see someone shouting in traffic, a shopkeeper fuming at a late delivery, or an uncle dramatically slapping his forehead during a family debate. It's not that people in Bangladesh are angrier-it's just that expressing it openly is more culturally accepted. Public frustration is part of the landscape, often expressed without shame and sometimes with flair.

Now contrast that with a British office. You won't see people raising their voices or stomping out of meetings. Instead, anger comes dressed in sarcasm or passive- aggressive remarks. Think eye rolls, loaded pauses, or a tight smile paired with a polite, "Well, that's one way to do it."

The people are expressing the same emotion in totally different ways.

Understanding these cultural differences matters, especially in a global work environment. What looks like inappropriate outburst in one culture might be considered honest communication in another. And what sounds like a snide remark might actually be a Western colleague trying to signal frustration . . . quietly.

How to Handle Anger Without Fueling the Fire

Let's be honest-anger is loud in Bangladesh. It's how many of us were raised to show urgency, frustration, or authority. But in Western workplaces, that same energy can backfire.

Here's the key: **Don't match the heat-cool it down.**

If you raise your voice or slam a hand on the table, it won't make you look passionate. It might make people nervous. Worse, it might make you seem unprofessional-even aggressive.

Instead, try these strategies that help you stay effective without losing your fire:

- **Listen before reacting.** Many people just want to feel heard. Let them speak before you step in.

- **Acknowledge feelings.** Try saying, "I can see you're frustrated." It shows you're tuned in, not tuned out.

- **Lower your volume.** You don't need to whisper - but keep your tone steady. Calm invites calm.

- **Pause, then respond.** Don't jump into blame or defense. Take a breath, then choose your words wisely.

- **Know when to ask for help.** If things feel too charged, bring in a neutral third party - like HR or a team lead.

In multicultural workplaces, different people express emotion differently. What feels "normal" to you might feel intense to someone else. Being aware of that difference allows you to temper your reactions better and match the expected tone, even when you feel your emotions starting to rise.

Strategies for Managing Anger

Now, you may also find yourself on the opposite end of this, having to handle someone else's anger. So, what do you do when frustration bubbles up, or when someone else's anger lands in your inbox?

1. **De - Escalation Techniques**

Keep calm and listen actively. Acknowledge the other person's feelings without jumping in to fix, defend, or deflect. Measured language, neutral tone, and steady body language can do wonders to lower the emotional temperature.

2. **Empathy and Cultural Sensitivity**

Pause to consider the backstory. What norms are shaping this person's emotional response? What might this expression of anger look like from their cultural perspective? A little empathy, especially the cross cultural kind, goes a long way.

3. **Professional Support**

If the situation becomes too complex to navigate alone, bring in a neutral third party. Human resources professionals or trained mediators are especially helpful when cultural misunderstandings add fuel to the fire.

Cross - Cultural Conflict in Action: Amir and Lucy

Let's walk through a real world example.

Amir, a Bangladeshi project manager, is collaborating with Lucy, a British colleague. A timeline slips, and Lucy, clearly annoyed, drops a sarcastic line during a team meeting: "Well, I guess we're just redefining what 'deadline' means now, aren't we?"

Amir, not reading the tension behind the tone, laughs, thinking it's a light joke.

Lucy, feeling dismissed, gets more irritated. Amir's confusion grows. Cue a spiral of miscommunication.

Thankfully, their manager steps in. Understanding both cultural perspectives, the manager facilitates a conversation. Lucy explains that her sarcasm was meant to express serious concern. Amir shares how sarcasm isn't commonly used in his culture and was genuinely unsure how to respond.

Through open dialogue, both parties walk away with greater clarity, and a renewed commitment to transparent communication.

Beyond anger, let's take a look at how you can handle some other common workplace issues in the West.

Understanding & Empathy vs. Solutions

Now let's explore one of the most common cultural and interpersonal speed bumps in the workplace.

Someone shares a problem with you.

You want to help. So you jump in with solutions:

"Why don't you just send a follow - up email?"
"You should talk to your boss."
"Next time, do this instead . . ."

But they don't look relieved. They look . . . disappointed.

What just happened?

You solved the problem, right?

Not quite.

Let's reveal the truth: sometimes, people don't need you to *solve* the problem. They need you to *see* the problem, with them in it.

This is where many well- meaning professionals, especially those raised to be "fixers" miss the mark. In Western workplaces, the instinct to jump in with solutions can backfire. It can come across as cold, rushed, or even dismissive.

But here's the shift that changes everything: **Listen first, then fix.**

When someone's venting about a bad meeting, a team conflict, or just a tough day, they're often asking silently:

- "Do you see how hard this was for me?"

- "Can I trust you enough to be honest with you?"

- "Will you just listen for a moment?"

If you answer with advice too quickly, even great advice, it's like handing them an umbrella when they're trying to explain the storm.

The Listening Blueprint

Here's how to move from "fixer" to trusted teammate:

1. **Resist the Fix - It's a Reflex**
   Just pause. Take a breath. Stay with the moment.

2. **Listen for Emotions, Not Just Events**
   Are they feeling ignored? Frustrated? Ashamed? Lost?

3. **Validate Their Feelings**
   Say things like:
   "That must have been frustrating."
   "I get why that would feel unfair."

4. **Ask Before Advising**
   "Do you want to talk through some ideas together?"
   "Would it help if I offered a few thoughts?"

Connection First. Solutions Second.

Once someone feels heard, they're more open to collaboration. Not just advice, but real, mutual problem solving. This approach builds emotional trust, which is the foundation of strong working relationship especially across cultures.

Listen to Understand, Not Just to Solve
Sometimes, the best support isn't a solution - it's simply being present. Before offering advice, take a moment to really listen to what the other person is feeling. When someone feels truly heard, they're more open, more trusting, and far more ready to solve the problem *with* you - not just be handed a fix.

Handling Criticism: A Cultural Reset

In many South Asian workplaces, including Bangladesh and India, criticism often comes top down. It may be blunt, emotional, and hierarchical. A manager might scold in front of others or use strong language to drive a point home. In such environments, feedback can feel like a verdict, and the safest response is silence or submission.

But in Western professional culture, criticism plays a very different role. It's usually framed as **feedback**, and while it can still sting, it's rarely meant to humiliate. Instead, it's positioned as part of growth. Even junior employees are encouraged to give upward feedback. And the healthiest teams don't avoid critique - they invite it.

Here's how to navigate this shift without losing your balance:

Don't Take It Personally
Western feedback often focuses on a specific behavior, not your identity. If someone says, "This report missed the key points," they're not attacking your intelligence - they're flagging something fixable.

Stay Open, Not Defensive
You might feel the urge to explain or justify. Pause. Listen. Then respond with curiosity: "Thanks for pointing that out can you tell me more about what you were expecting?"

Ask for Clarity
If the feedback feels vague, don't be afraid to ask: "What could I do differently next time?" This shows initiative and makes it easier to act on the input.

Remember: Silence Isn't Respect Here
In some cultures, silence shows humility. But in Western contexts, silence can look like disinterest. Even a simple "Thanks, I'll work on that" shows you're engaged and willing to grow.

In Western settings, criticism isn't an insult – it's a tool.
Used well, it sharpens your skills and deepens trust with your team.

Handling Deflection (Whataboutism) in Discussions

If you've ever tried to discuss an issue, only to have the other person immediately pivot to something *completely* different – congrats! You've been hit with a classic move called **whataboutism**.

It sounds like this:

"I'm concerned about the delivery delay."
"Well, what about the payment schedule? That's never been fair."

Cue internal screaming.

What Is Whataboutism, Really?

Whataboutism is that slippery little tactic people use to dodge accountability or derail the conversation. It throws a completely different issue into the mix, often one that sounds *sort of* related but isn't really the point. It's like bringing up your childhood dentist in the middle of a divorce discussion. Confusing, misdirected, and let's be honest kind of annoying.

This form of deflection can show up in political debates, workplace discussions, and international negotiations alike. And if you're not careful, it'll suck the focus right out of the room.

Case in Point: Fatima vs. The Pivot King

Meet Fatima, a detail oriented professional from Dhaka. She's in a virtual negotiation call with Stefan, a procurement lead from Germany. They're going over the final terms for a vendor contract.

Fatima calmly raises a red flag:

"We're concerned about your delivery timeline - it's too tight for our project cycle."

Without missing a beat, Stefan fires back:

"Well, what about the payment terms? You've been delaying those for months."

And just like that, poof - the original issue is off the table.

But not on Fatima's watch.

Instead of letting the conversation spiral, she nods and says, "I hear you on the payment terms. Let's schedule time to go over that tomorrow. But for now, let's make sure the delivery schedule works for both of us. It's critical for our planning."

Boom. Calm. Direct. Respectful. She acknowledged the concern, promised to return to it, and *then* brought everyone back on track.

Strategies for Addressing Whataboutism:

So, How Do You Tame the Whataboutism Beast?

1. Acknowledge, Then Pivot

You don't want to ignore the other person's point entirely, that just creates defensiveness. Instead, validate briefly, then guide the conversation back.

"That's a fair point - we should definitely talk about that. But right now, let's finish resolving [insert original topic]."

2. State the Purpose

Sometimes people drift off - topic because they lose sight of why you're even talking.

"To stay aligned with our goals today, we need to wrap up the delivery timeline discussion first. That's our top priority."

3. Park It - Don't Bury It

If the raised issue matters, suggest setting it aside for a different meeting. Keep a visible "parking lot" list if needed.

"Let's table that for Thursday's meeting. I'll make sure it's the first thing on the agenda."

When handled well, deflection doesn't have to derail anything. In fact, showing that you can calmly steer the conversation back to the point, while still respecting the other party, makes you look like the true professional in the room.

> **Whataboutism** is like arguing about the umbrella while standing in the rain. Address the storm first, and then talk accessories."

The Anatomy of a Real Apology

You may eventually find yourself in a situation where you need to apologize, even if it wasn't fully your fault. In Western professional culture, a good apology isn't about shame, it's about ownership. When something goes wrong, even unintentionally, a sincere apology can preserve trust and show emotional intelligence.

Here's the key: a professional apology focuses on impact, not intent.

- **Don't over explain:** "I didn't mean to" can sound defensive.

- **Acknowledge the effect:** "I see how that caused confusion."

- **Keep it simple and sincere:** "I'm sorry for missing the deadline. I understand it caused delays, and I'm taking steps to make sure it doesn't happen again."

- **Follow through:** A true apology includes action.

Used well, an apology is not a weakness. It's a signal of maturity, accountability, and respect - qualities that are highly valued in any work environment.

"A real apology doesn't start with excuses - it starts with empathy."
It's not about being wrong. It's about making it right.

Turning Conflict into Connection

Conflict is inevitable, especially in diverse, fast paced workplaces. But it doesn't have to derail trust or damage your reputation. In fact, how you handle criticism, conflict, and apologies can become one of your greatest professional strengths.

The key is to respond, not react. To stay grounded when others get heated. To recognize when a genuine apology can rebuild what criticism might have cracked.

Criticism isn't always an attack. Conflict isn't always a failure. And an apology isn't a weakness - it's a bridge back to mutual respect.

With emotional control, cultural awareness, and a bit of humility, you can turn tense moments into turning points. That's not just good professionalism, it's great leadership.

PART 3:

∾

OVERCOMING WORKPLACE CHALLENGES

CHAPTER 5:
NAVIGATING BIAS, DISCRIMINATION, AND CONFLICT

"Where Are You Really From?"

I remember walking into my first job interview in the UK with a crisp suit, a hopeful heart, and a last - minute Google search on how to give a proper handshake.

The interviewer smiled, gestured for me to sit, and asked the usual ice-breaker.

"So, where are you from?"

"London," I said, with a grin.

"No, no - I mean, where are you *really* from?"

There it was.

It wasn't the first time I'd heard it. And it wouldn't be the last. But that question, full of hidden assumptions and a subtle sense of "you don't belong" - reminded me that succeeding here wouldn't just be about showing my skills. It would also mean learning to navigate hidden bias.

That moment stayed with me, not because it was openly offensive, but because it quietly revealed how easily people can fall into biased thinking without even noticing.

In Western societies, especially in countries like the UK, the US, Canada, and Australia-the fight against discrimination has been long and complicated. From racism and sexism to ageism, and homophobia, these cultures have wrestled with systemic biases for generations. While real progress has been made, the work is far from over.

And if you're working in these environments - whether in- person or remotely - **understanding the history and context behind these issues isn't optional**. It's essential.

During my early years in the UK, racial discrimination was not subtle. Sexism wasn't hidden. These issues were out in the open, and though society has since taken significant steps forward, the scars - and the sensitivities remain.

That's why this chapter isn't just about what *not* to do. It's about how to **understand**, **adapt**, and **show up with empathy** in a workplace that takes equity seriously.

The Foundation of Respect

Every conversation about discrimination starts here:
Everyone deserves respect.

When discrimination shows up, whether through words, assumptions, or silence, it signals a failure to honor that core principle.

And here's the key: respect isn't just about being polite. It's about learning to see the **full humanity** of the people you work with. This includes their backgrounds, beliefs, identities, and lived experiences matter, not just socially, but professionally.

This doesn't mean you have to become an expert in every global issue. But it *does* mean you need to be curious, open, and willing to learn.

Start by asking yourself:

- What parts of my background might others not understand?

- What might I be missing about theirs?

It could be as simple as helping a colleague learn how to pronounce your name or taking the time to learn theirs. Sharing what your name means, telling why you celebrate certain holidays, or even explaining a gesture that might seem unfamiliar to others can turn confusion into connection.

Speak Up, Professionally

If you encounter discrimination, toward yourself or someone else, know this: **you are not alone**, and you should speak up about it.

Most Western workplaces have formal systems for reporting and resolving issues related to discrimination. HR departments and senior leadership teams are expected to protect a safe, inclusive environment. Use those systems.

Raising a concern isn't a disruption. It's **part of the culture**.

When you speak up, you're not just protecting yourself, you're helping create a space where others feel safe to be fully themselves too.

Names Matter. Pronouns Matter. Titles Matter.

In a global team, names are more than identifiers, they're part of our story. Yet, mispronunciation happens, a lot.

Some people are forgiving. Others, not so much. And honestly? Both reactions are valid.

Making an effort to get someone's name right is a **small gesture with big impact**. Even if you fumble at first, trying counts. In fact, trying often matters more than getting it perfect.

That's why many professionals from countries like India or Bangladesh adopt simplified names or nicknames in international settings. Usually, this is not a personal choice, but a practical trade - off that shows how much emotional effort goes into simply trying to belong. And names are just the beginning.

In today's workplace, especially in Western societies, being mindful of **pronouns** and **titles** is increasingly important. If someone tells you their pronouns are "they/them," using them isn't optional - it's **respectful**.

Same with academic or professional titles that hold meaning: "Dr.," "Professor," "Reverend," or cultural honorifics. Get them right. They matter.

Whether it's a name, a pronoun, or a cultural tradition, learning how to **acknowledge someone fully** is a basic part of being an effective teammate.

Sexism

Let's be real: sexism didn't vanish after the last HR slideshow.

Even with all the awareness campaigns and diversity pledges, it is still present - in boardrooms, in passive comments during meetings, and in those everyday moments when something just feels wrong.

And here's the uncomfortable truth: in many Western settings, sexism persists not only because of active discrimination but because of passive **ignorance**. Even well meaning professionals sometimes don't realize when they're perpetuating gender based bias.

To make sure we aren't adding to this problem, let's walk through a few real world scenarios, each demonstrating a different degree of sexism that shows up in professional spaces:

Case 1: The Overprotective Team Leader

She was the new hire, fresh, talented, and full of ideas. Her manager? He took it upon himself to be her "shield."

It started innocently enough "Don't worry, I'll talk to them for you." Then came, "Just run everything through me first, okay?" And finally, "I'd rather you not meet with them alone."

At first, it might have looked like support. But over time, it morphed into something else entirely: **control**.

Instead of empowering her to build relationships across the team, he became her sole point of contact. She had no direct communication, no visibility, and no autonomy within the team.

Here's the issue:
Protectiveness that limits someone's professional independence isn't protection - it's **patronizing control in disguise**.

Case 2: Unsolicited Gifts

He said it was friendly, a "welcome to the team" gesture.
But the flowers arrived without warning. Then came the messages. Then another small gift.

She barely knew him.

What he saw as charm, she felt as pressure. There was no invitation, no clear context, and certainly no desire for romantic attention at work. Now, instead of focusing on her new role, she was wondering how to avoid him without creating tension.

Here's the issue:
Gifts, when unsolicited and personal, create ambiguity - and that ambiguity leads to discomfort. Especially when power dynamics are involved. What feels "sweet" to one person may feel **awkward, intrusive, and inappropriate** to another.

Case 3: Disrespect of Personal Space

Every office has one, someone who stands too close, touches others too much, or leans in just a little too far during every conversation, even after you've stepped back.

This kind of boundary pushing might not seem like a big deal to the person doing it, but to the person experiencing it, it is uncomfortable.

Here's the issue:
Personal space doesn't just include physical space, it includes **emotional and psychological safety** too. Ignoring someone's cues, even subtle ones, shows a lack of respect. And repeated boundary crossing becomes **harassment**, not habit.

Case 4: Stalking Behavior

It starts as a Slack message about a meeting. Then a LinkedIn comment. Then a personal email. Then texts. Then showing up at your lunch spot. Suddenly, it's no longer about work.

This is what workplace stalking can look like. It doesn't have to be peeking in someone's window or following them home. Sometimes it's disguised as "just being friendly" or "trying to get to know you."

But when the communication becomes **relentless, uninvited, and clearly non-work related**, it crosses the line.

Here's the issue:
Stalking behavior invades privacy, shatters trust, and makes the workplace feel **unsafe**. Victims often stay silent because they fear backlash, being blamed, or not being believed.

Why These Stories Matter

You might read these and think, "But I would never do that." Great. But here's the deeper point:

Would you notice if someone else did?
Would you know how to intervene?

Would you recognize the signs before someone else had to explain them?

Sexism isn't always obvious. Sometimes it is hidden in unchecked power, familiar habits, and assumptions that no one ever questions. But the impact is the same: it limits potential, erodes trust, and drives talented people away.

The way to change it is to be aware, speak up, and take action when you see it happening.

Next, we'll continue exploring how Western workplaces handle these challenges and how you can navigate and address them.

General Considerations: Why It's Never "Just a Joke"

In every one of the previous cases from overstepping team leaders to boundary, blurring colleagues, there's one common thread: the attention is **unwanted**.

When a workplace interaction causes someone discomfort, embarrassment, or distress, especially on a repeated basis - it's not harmless. It's harassment.

No matter how "small" it may seem at first, the emotional cost adds up. People feel watched instead of valued, silenced instead of seen. Once that kind of dynamic creeps into a team, it poisons trust, stalls collaboration, and drives good people away.

That's why workplaces need more than a written policy in their employee handbook. They need active systems, real, visible support that gives people the tools and courage to speak up.

As a team leader, I've made it a point to **proactively support the women on my teams**, not just when things go wrong, but by creating a culture where issues can be raised *before* they become problems.

Most of the time, the challenges don't come from bad intentions, they come from people who don't yet understand the culture they've stepped into. That's why early conversations matter. Waiting for a pattern to form is too late.

The key? Address it quickly, clearly, and respectfully. You're not just managing behavior, you're shaping the standard.

Handling Sexism and Sexual Harassment in the Workplace

Sexism in the workplace isn't always aggressive. Sometimes, it's in the design of the break room, the unspoken assumptions in a meeting, or the jokes that everyone nervously laughs at but no one actually enjoys.

It shows up when there's no accessible restroom for non male colleagues.
When career opportunities consistently go to one gender over another. When someone's presence is reduced to commentary on their appearance instead of their performance.

Often, people don't realize they're part of the problem. But that doesn't change the impact.

If you experience sexism or notice it happening around you, here's what to know:

First, recognize it.
Sexism can be subtle, especially in workplaces where it's gone unchecked for a long time. But if you feel a consistent sense of exclusion, discomfort, or disrespect tied to your gender, trust that instinct.
Second, speak up.
That doesn't always mean confronting someone directly. Start with someone you trust. Raise it with a manager or an HR representative. Keep notes. Be clear. Good leaders will take it seriously - even if they're surprised at first.

Now let's address the heavier side of this issue: **sexual harassment**.

This includes unwanted sexual comments, advances, gestures, or behavior. And, no, it doesn't matter what you were wearing, how you smiled, or how friendly you were. The responsibility lies entirely with the harasser.

If you're ever in this situation, here's what I advise-based on experience, training, and years of supporting others through it:

How to Respond to Sexual Harassment

1. **Prioritize Your Safety**
   You don't have to handle this alone. Discreetly reach out to trusted allies-colleagues, friends, mentors-who can support you. Just talking about what's happening can take the weight off your shoulders and help you see things more clearly.

2. **Keep Records**
   Start a detailed log. Write down what happened, when, and where. Note the language used, the context, and how it made you feel. If others witnessed it, ask if they'd be willing to write down what they saw. These notes may be crucial if things escalate.

3. **If Safe, Address It Directly (But Only If You Choose To)**
   Sometimes, a direct conversation is possible. If you decide to go this route, bring a trusted colleague. Stay calm, and speak clearly: "Your behavior is inappropriate, and I need it to stop." You can also inform them that the matter has been reported and that further escalation will follow if it continues.

4. **Escalate as Needed**
   If the behavior persists or retaliation begins, escalate. Speak to HR, document their responses, and involve senior leaders. Let your professionalism be your power. Even if the journey is long, it's worth protecting yourself and others.

Be Prepared for Any Outcome

Ideally, the harassment stops, you receive an apology, and things improve.

But not every workplace is perfect. You might face pushback or resistance or find that the person in question has more influence than expected. You may need to switch teams-or in some cases, walk away entirely.

Leaving is hard. But enduring ongoing harassment is harder.

In the most difficult cases, the harasser may try to **deflect, deny, or discredit**. That's why your calm persistence, documentation, and support network are so essential.

And remember: **you are not alone**.

There are resources out there legal support, hotlines, online communities, HR allies-waiting to walk with you through the storm.

Harassment Is Never Your Fault
If someone harasses you, it's not because of what you wore, said, or did. It's because they crossed a line. Harassment is about control, not clothing. Your job is not to feel shame - it's to stay safe and speak up.

Equality and Equity

If you've ever seen that now famous illustration of three people of different heights trying to look over a fence, each standing on the same sized box, you know the punchline.

Equality gives everyone the same box.
Equity gives everyone what they need to actually see over the fence.

That's the difference.

WESTERN PROFESSIONALISM BENGALI ROOTS

In global teams and diverse workplaces, it's not enough to treat everyone the same. We have to create environments where everyone has a fair chance - not just in theory, but in practice.

That may mean someone needs extra support, more flexibility, or a different type of accommodation to succeed. And that's not special treatment. That's **equity** in action.

But here's the flip side: just as we learn to be aware of others' needs, we also need to advocate for our own. Share what helps you thrive, whether it's flexible hours, clear feedback, or support navigating cultural dynamics. **You're part of the equity conversation too.**

Ageism: The Quiet Bias That Hides in Politeness

Ageism isn't always cruel or obvious. Sometimes it comes wrapped in politeness, tradition, or compliments that carry unintended weight.

In Southeast Asian cultures, age often plays a central role in how we communicate. Our languages even come with built in titles and honorifics to reflect age differences, a system meant to promote respect. And it does, beautifully.

But here's where it becomes problematic: that respect can sometimes morph into **rigid hierarchy**. Younger people may feel invisible. Older people may be idealized or excluded. Either way, it becomes harder to connect as equals.

In Western cultures, ageism tends to show up differently - especially in hiring. Older professionals are often passed over because of unspoken assumptions: "They're too slow," "too expensive," or "not adaptable enough."

At the same time, there's a kind of *reverse ageism* too, where younger employees are brushed aside as inexperienced or immature, regardless of their ideas or impact.

And then there's the "wisdom trap": the idea that wisdom automatically increases with age. It sounds flattering, but it also creates flaws in our thinking, limiting how we view others and ourselves.

Here's the truth: capability doesn't wear a specific age. Wisdom doesn't come with a number. And innovation can spark from any corner of the room.

So, what can we do?

Challenge the stereotypes. Age should never equate to value.

Support intergenerational collaboration. Mentorship can and should go both ways.

Promote skills, not age brackets. Look at what people bring to the table, not how long they've been alive.

Creating an inclusive team means making space for everyone, whether they're fresh out of school or nearing retirement. Age shouldn't be a barrier. It should be another dimension of the richness we bring to our work.

Ableism: The Discrimination We Don't Always See

Ableism can show up in things like needed ramps that are missing from buildings, meetings without captions, and software that assumes everyone can see, hear, or type.

It can also show up in things like assumptions, policies designed only for "typical" employees, and the surprised tone of voice when someone with a disability excels.

At its core, ableism is about prioritizing able bodied norms and ignoring the incredible diversity of minds, bodies, and ways of experiencing the world.

If we want to build inclusive workplaces, we have to go beyond compliance. We need to **actively design for inclusion**, physically, digitally, emotionally, and socially.

Here's how we start:

- **Education and awareness:** Host workshops, share stories, break the silence.

- **Accessibility:** Apply universal design principles everywhere, offices, websites, tools, and schedules.

- **Inclusive policies:** Offer flexibility, adjust roles, listen when someone tells you what they need.

- **Representation and voice:** Let individuals with disabilities lead the conversation, not just be included in it.

- **Break the narrative:** Celebrate people with disabilities not *despite* their challenges, but for the full scope of their contributions.

True inclusion doesn't mean "fitting people in." It means **redesigning the system so it works for everyone**.

Respect as a Daily Practice

Whether we're talking about gender, age, ability, race, religion, or identity, the principle is the same: **everyone deserves dignity. Everyone deserves opportunity.**

Discrimination takes many forms, but they all draw the same line: *you don't belong.*

Our job, as professionals in a global workplace, is to erase that line daily, through listening, learning, speaking up, and showing up with empathy.

This goes beyond HR compliance to true leadership.

You don't need a title to make a difference. You just need the willingness to see people clearly, advocate for fairness, and hear others' stories, especially when they're different from your own.

This is key to excelling in the Western business environment, where you will likely encounter a wide range of people and need to interact with them professionally.

Now let's talk about a few deeper ways you can more readily adapt to Western culture.

CHAPTER 6:
ADAPTING WELL TO WESTERN CULTURE

Rina's Boardroom Balancing Act

When Rina landed a job at a San Francisco tech startup, she was thrilled. After earning her MBA, she was ready to take on the world or at least the world of SaaS and Slack threads. The office was open concept, kombucha flowed freely, and her onboarding included a workshop titled Deconstructing Power Structures in Agile Workflows.

It was a lot.

At first, Rina absorbed everything easily. She nodded during heated discussions about "late stage capitalism," reposted infographics about corporate activism, and tried her best to blend in. She didn't want to seem rigid or "too traditional." But under the surface, she had questions.

Why did everyone speak in extremes?
Why was disagreeing quietly seen as passivity, or worse, complicity?

Then came the all hands meeting.

The CEO gave a passionate speech about dismantling hierarchies and how "everyone is a leader here." It sounded inspiring, but Rina noticed something odd: the same three people dominated every conversation and they weren't exactly junior.

Later that week, she mentioned this casually to her mentor, an Indian - American product lead named Anjali. Anjali smiled knowingly.

"Rina," she said, "don't mistake style for substance. There's a lot of posturing in Western workplaces, performative equality, performative outrage, even performative humility. You've got to see through the packaging."

That hit hard.

Rina realized she had been treating every TED Talk, team building workshop, and LinkedIn post like gospel truth. But just like back home, every message had a motive, and sometimes, a marketing budget.

So she started **thinking critically**. She began asking: *Who benefits from this message? What's not being said? Is this real inclusion, or just optics?*

At the same time, she didn't shut herself off. She respected the workplace culture, she participated, adapted, and even led but with her eyes open and her values intact.

Instead of mimicking extremes, she brought **balance**. When discussions turned reactive, she offered perspective. When a junior teammate from Nigeria felt too afraid to speak up, Rina pulled her into the conversation. When management proposed a flashy DEI initiative with no real follow through, she raised thoughtful questions, privately and respectfully.

Over time, colleagues began to trust her, not just for her ideas, but for her integrity. She wasn't just another employee blending in. She became a cultural translator, a calm presence in chaotic meetings, and someone who could *see the game without playing it blindly*.

She didn't just fit into the culture - she elevated it.

Adaptation is a Skill of Blending, Not Conforming

Success in a Western environment does not mean abandoning your cultural identity. It's a nuanced balance of maintaining your strengths while embracing new ways of working. True cultural competence is about blending, not conforming.

Adapting Without Losing Yourself

You've probably heard this advice before: "When in Rome, do as the Romans do." It sounds wise, until you realize the Romans might be doing some pretty confusing things.

In Western work culture, adapting can feel like walking a tightrope. On one side, there's the pressure to "fit in" to speak up boldly, challenge ideas in meetings, and keep up with cultural references about shows you've never seen. On the other side, there's the fear of going too far and losing the parts of yourself that make you . . . you.

This chapter is about finding the **middle path**.

You'll learn how to adapt thoughtfully, **not by blindly agreeing or rebelling**, but by recognizing cultural messaging (yes, even the subtle propaganda), thinking critically, and choosing which values to embrace and which to question. You'll discover how to respect the culture you're in *without being swallowed by it* and how to stand tall in a room full of people without shouting just to be heard.

Whether it's a Netflix series, a team building seminar, or a bold opinion on Slack, Western environments are full of strong narratives. But you don't have to absorb them all. You can be informed, engaged, and adaptable, *without being edited*.

Let's talk about how.

Recognizing Propaganda and Political Nuances

The Mysterious "News" Forward

It started with a WhatsApp forward. Rezaul clicked the link out of habit, another flashy headline claiming, "Foreign Investors Pulling Out of Bangladesh Overnight!" The source? A suspicious website ending in ".buzz." The article was peppered with capital letters, red fonts, and lots of finger pointing. He read it twice before forwarding it to his team group chat. Within ten minutes, panic set in. One teammate asked if their client deal was in danger. Another declared they should move money into USD immediately.

Later that day, over coffee with his manager, Rezaul sheepishly admitted he hadn't verified the story. His manager smiled and said, "Welcome to the age of weaponized information. Next time, check the source before you light a fire."

Definition and History of Propaganda

Propaganda isn't just a relic of wartime posters or black and white broadcasts. It's alive and well, in memes, headlines, viral videos, and cleverly designed media clips. At its core, **propaganda is the systematic effort to shape public opinion or behavior** through selective messaging.

Whether from governments, organizations, or individuals, the goal is the same: influence. Sometimes it's blatant; often it's subtle. For professionals, especially those working across borders and cultures, the ability to *recognize* propaganda is just as vital as the ability to communicate clearly.

The Art of Thinking Critically

For Bangladeshi professionals navigating global landscapes, critical thinking isn't optional it's a survival skill. In a world of conflicting headlines and algorithm, shaped opinions, the question isn't just, "Is this true?" but, "Who benefits from me believing this?"

Developing critical thinking means practicing intellectual curiosity with healthy skepticism.

Ask: Who's the source? What's their motive? Is there evidence, or just emotion? Is the language inflammatory or measured? Propaganda often relies on logical fallacies and emotional triggers, which you can spot if you know what to look for.

Workshops, seminars, and media literacy training, especially those that focus on international communication, are excellent tools. Online platforms now offer resources that sharpen the ability to detect bias, decode loaded language, and challenge manipulative narratives. The more you practice, the better your "radar" becomes.

Dialogue: The Antidote to Manipulation

One of the best defenses against propaganda? **Open dialogue.** Diverse conversations reveal blind spots. When we surround ourselves with people who think differently, colleagues from other regions, clients with opposing political leanings, or even mentors from different generations, we create space for thoughtful disagreement. These moments sharpen our judgment, making us less susceptible to easy answers or emotional manipulation.

Case Study: Training the Filter

At a multinational company with a diverse workforce, leadership noticed a troubling trend: employees were reacting strongly to polarizing news headlines. Some started spreading misinformation, unaware it was part of a larger propaganda campaign. In response, the company launched a **media literacy training program** tailored for a global team, including Bangladeshi professionals.

The program didn't just focus on "fake news." It taught employees how to spot biased framing, emotional language, and manipulative visuals. Through group exercises, real time examples, and role playing, participants learned to pause, question, and analyze. The result? A workforce that didn't just consume information - they evaluated it.

In a world where influence is sold by the click, mastering the art of discernment is more than intellectual, it's strategic. Professionals who can recognize propaganda won't just protect their credibility; they'll lead with clarity, steer through noise, and foster cultures grounded in truth.

Cultural Expressions Through Art and Activities

The Dance That Changed the Project

When Maya signed up for the company's cultural workshop, she expected a few awkward introductions and maybe a sampling of international snacks. What she didn't expect was to find herself, two hours later, trying to master a traditional West African dance routine alongside her Bangladeshi, Brazilian, and Japanese colleagues. She fumbled through the steps, laughing at her own stiff arms while being coached by Samuel from HR, who, to everyone's surprise, moved like he belonged on stage.

By the end of the workshop, something shifted. Conversations flowed more easily, team members cheered each other on in meetings, and collaboration across departments, something previously strained, began to feel more natural. One dance, one moment of cultural immersion, had bridged months of hesitation.

Art is more than beauty or decoration, it's a living expression of culture. Whether it's a haunting melody, an intricate dance, a wall of graffiti, or a classic poem, each artistic form tells a story about the values, struggles, history, and spirit of people. For professionals working across borders, engaging with the art of that culture offers a gateway to understanding what language alone cannot convey.

Art as a Cultural Decoder

Bangladeshi professionals expanding into global teams can build cultural empathy through direct engagement with local expressions. Attend festivals. Watch traditional performances. Read literature in translation. Visit galleries, both modern and traditional. These are not leisure activities, they're informal classrooms where culture speaks its truth.

It's not just about passive appreciation either. Ask yourself: "What influenced this art form? What historical events shaped it? What emotions does it carry that aren't said out loud?" Understanding these layers adds emotional intelligence to your cultural fluency, and people feel that.

From Canvas to Collaboration: Practical Ways to Engage

Take a Class

Sign up for a traditional dance or painting workshop. You'll not only gain insight into non verbal communication, but you'll also better appreciate the aesthetics that matter to your colleagues from different backgrounds. Even a short session on calligraphy or drumming can open your eyes to rhythm, precision, and cultural pride that influence communication styles.

Join Cultural Exchange Programs

Whether virtual or in person, these programs offer immersive experiences that go beyond surface level interactions. You'll experience real stories, food, rituals, and conversations that humanize the culture behind the title on the business card.

Cross - Cultural Competence: A Path Forward

I once coached a young Bangladeshi analyst named Afsana who had just landed her first overseas posting in Morocco. She was bright, well prepared, and armed with every business protocol guide she could find online. Still, she was completely thrown off during her first team meeting when everyone started talking over each other - and then laughed and hugged after. "Were they arguing?" she asked me, bewildered. In fact, they were excited. She soon learned that in Moroccan team culture, animated debates are a sign of passion and camaraderie. Once she stopped trying to control the chaos and started joining it, her work relationships flourished. What she thought was a culture clash was just a **rhythm she hadn't learned to dance to yet.**

That's the heart of cross cultural competence: learning new rhythms without losing your own beat. The world doesn't need clones, it needs collaborators who understand when to lead, when to listen, and how to bridge the gaps in between.

The most successful global professionals aren't just fluent in English, Excel, or email etiquette. They're fluent in **people,** in the cultural cues, unspoken norms, and subtle rhythms that shape human interaction across borders. Developing cross cultural competence goes far beyond memorizing a list of dos and don'ts. It's a posture of curiosity, a willingness to observe, reflect, and adapt. For Bangladeshi professionals navigating international spaces, this skill isn't optional, it's a **superpower**.

That superpower is built one experience at a time: sitting in on meetings in Tokyo, navigating small talk in São Paulo, decoding silence in Nairobi, or learning when a smile in Stockholm means "yes" and when it means "no, but politely." Each moment sharpens your sensitivity and expands your range.

Want to build this muscle? Start where you are. Join community groups that reflect different cultures. Find mentors who've worked internationally and ask for their best stories, and their worst mistakes. Look for opportunities to work on global projects, even remotely. The more exposure you get, the more fluent you become in understanding people who see the world differently.

PART 4:

LEADERSHIP AND
PROFESSIONAL GROWTH

CHAPTER 7:
PROFESSIONAL MANAGEMENT, LEADERSHIP, AND COMMUNICATION

The Manager Who Wouldn't Let Go

When Adiba landed her first job at an international marketing firm in Dhaka, she was eager to prove herself. Fresh out of university, she was assigned to a team led by Mr. Karim, a manager with a reputation for being well, let's say *hands - on*.

From the start, Adiba noticed that every email, design draft, or client message she prepared was closely reviewed, edited, and often rewritten by Mr. Karim. At first, she took it as part of the learning curve. But weeks passed, then months, and the micromanagement didn't let up. Team members weren't just guided, they were shadowed. Suggestions were shut down. Decisions were already made before meetings began.

"I'm not learning," Adiba confided in a coworker over tea one afternoon. "I'm just executing orders. I could be replaced by a checklist."

Eventually, Mr. Karim's rigid approach began to take a toll. The team, stifled by the lack of autonomy, started missing deadlines, not because they were unmotivated, but because everything had to funnel through one person. Creativity flatlined. Turnover rose.

It wasn't until a new regional director stepped in and introduced peer led projects and open brainstorming sessions that things began to shift. Mr. Karim was encouraged to attend leadership coaching and slowly began embracing a different model, one where he asked more than he instructed and listened more than he corrected.

Adiba's next campaign pitch was approved on the first go. "I trusted your process," Mr. Karim said simply. "Let's build on it." That moment marked not just a win for Adiba, but a turning point for the whole team.

This chapter explores what that shift looks like, from managing tasks to managing people, from control to collaboration. Whether you're just starting your career or already guiding others, understanding how to lead and be led with intention is critical in today's global workplace.

Communication and Clarity in Leadership

Strong leadership isn't just about what you say. It is about what others *hear*.

In diverse workplaces, especially those with a blend of Bangladeshi and Western professionals, how you *say* something matters just as much as *what* you say. Some teammates crave directness: "Just tell me what needs fixing." Others prefer a softer approach that preserves dignity and avoids confrontation. Both want clarity. But how they interpret tone, timing, and even silence is where the message can get lost

As a leader, you must adapt your style to those you lead. Listen more than you speak. Clarify instead of assuming. Understand that what feels assertive in one culture might sound blunt, or even rude, in another. And that what sounds polite in your head might land as vague or indecisive to someone else.

Great leaders don't stick to one communication style. They are observant and flexible. They build bridges with their words, because trust isn't built on eloquence alone, but on the feeling that you understand each other.

Responsibility and Ownership

As you move into a leadership role, your responsibilities change. It is no longer just about doing your own work well. It is also about helping others do their work effectively. This includes planning ahead, solving problems early, and offering consistent support to the team.

In leadership, ownership is not about receiving praise. It is about accepting responsibility. When something goes wrong, good leaders do not blame others. Instead, they ask, "What could I have done to support the team better?" This kind of thinking helps build trust. It also creates a work environment where people feel safe to share ideas, admit mistakes, and try new solutions.

For Bangladeshi professionals working in international or multicultural teams, it is important to understand that different cultures view accountability in different ways. In some workplaces, responsibility is focused on the individual. In others, it is shared by the group. A strong leader understands both approaches and helps the team know what is expected.

The goal is to make sure every team member understands their role and feels confident to contribute. Leadership is not just about giving instructions, it is about making sure the whole team can succeed.

Navigating Conflict with Professionalism

Conflict is a normal part of any workplace. When handled well, it can lead to better ideas, stronger teamwork, and more clarity about goals. But in cross cultural teams, people often have different ways of dealing with conflict.

Some professionals prefer to address problems directly. Others avoid open disagreement to protect relationships. In Bangladeshi culture, it is common to be indirect, especially with someone in a higher position.

This is often a way of showing respect. In many Western workplaces, however, direct communication and open debate are seen as useful and honest. Because of these differences, one person's silence may be misunderstood as agreement, or another person's direct comment may seem rude.

Leaders need to understand these differences and help their teams communicate clearly and respectfully. They can do this by offering safe ways to share feedback, such as anonymous surveys, private meetings, or follow up discussions after a project ends. These tools help uncover concerns that may not be shared openly and make space for better understanding.

Managing conflict in a healthy way builds trust and helps the team work better together.

Leading Across Cultures

Leadership today is not limited to one location or one way of doing things. Many professionals now work in global or multicultural teams. To lead well in these settings, it is important to develop *cultural intelligence,* the ability to understand, respect, and adjust to different cultural norms.

A culturally intelligent leader does not ignore or erase differences. Instead, they learn how to work with them. They stay curious, ask thoughtful questions, and try to understand others' points of view. For example, they may ask:

- How does this person understand leadership and authority?

- What kind of communication makes them feel comfortable?

- How can I respect their cultural background and still meet the expectations of our team?

This kind of awareness helps create a workplace where everyone feels respected and included. It also helps teams use their different perspectives to solve problems and make better decisions.

Understanding Management Styles

In the past, many managers led by giving strict orders and expecting everyone to follow without question. This style is known as *authoritarian leadership*. It focuses on control, clear rules, and top down decision-making. While this approach can make decisions faster, it often creates pressure and limits creativity. Team members may not feel comfortable sharing ideas or giving honest feedback.

In today's workplace, especially in the West and in knowledge based environments, this old style of leadership is becoming less effective. People want more than instructions, they want to be trusted, supported, and heard.

That's where *servant leadership* comes in.

A servant leader focuses on helping the team succeed. They ask questions like, "What do you need from me?" and, "How can I support your goals?" They give clear direction, but they also encourage independence. They listen, provide feedback, and help people grow in their roles.

This kind of leadership builds stronger teams. It helps people feel confident, respected, and motivated to do their best work. And instead of managing through fear or control, servant leaders create a culture of trust and cooperation.

For professionals working in international or cross cultural teams, understanding these differences in leadership style is important. Many Western workplaces now expect leaders to be supportive, not strict. Learning how to balance guidance with trust is an important step in becoming a strong leader in any setting.

Delegation: The Not - So - Secret Weapon

Being a strong manager isn't about having all the answers. It's about knowing who on your team *might* and empowering them to run with it.

Delegation isn't just about handing off tasks to lighten your load. It's about activating someone's zone of genius. When you trust a team member to tackle a complex challenge, you're telling them: "I believe in your judgment." And that belief, more than a task list, builds confidence, loyalty, and ownership.

And, yes, young professionals may start out waiting for instructions like they're still in school. That's normal. But the real goal isn't to spoon feed steps, it's to help them *build the recipe*. Senior managers who lead well will guide them from, "Tell me what to do," to, "Here's what I think we should try." That is an important shift.

Effective management isn't just about making sure things get done, it's about unlocking the full potential of the people doing them. The best managers don't just oversee work; they orchestrate it, pulling together diverse skills and sharp minds to solve real world problems. Think of it less like a chessboard and more like jazz, everyone has a part to play, and the magic happens when individuals are trusted to improvise with their expertise.

"Signs You're Leading, Not Bossing":
You ask more questions than you give orders.
You trust your team to make decisions.
You share credit generously.
You focus on *outcomes*, not controlling every step.

Delegation, in this context, becomes a kind of superpower. It's not about dumping tasks or ticking boxes, it's about saying, "I trust you to think, not just to do." When team members are empowered to use their judgment and stretch their skills, they not only produce better outcomes, they feel a real sense of ownership. That's when teams move from "functioning" to *thriving*.

Now, if you're just starting out in your career, it's easy to think your job is to simply follow instructions. Many of us were taught that success meant doing exactly what we were told. But the workplace is evolving. Good leaders aren't looking for robotic compliance, they're building future leaders. So, yes, they'll offer guidance. But what they're really hoping for is this: that you'll take that guidance and turn it into something even better. Not a checklist follower. A value adding contributor.

Navigating Expectation Management

Imagine this: You're midway through a team project when your manager suddenly asks for an update. You rattle off three bullet points and feel proud . . . only to be met with a blank stare and the dreaded question: "Why didn't I hear about this sooner?"

Cue the awkward pause.

Expectation management is the unglamorous but essential backbone of any successful professional relationship. Whether you're managing a team or being managed, knowing *what* to communicate, *when*, and *how much* can make the difference between smooth sailing and a shipwreck of misunderstandings.

Let's start with the basics: **Transparency.** Managers generally aren't mind readers (even if some pretend to be). They expect to be looped in early and often on major decisions, problems, and updates. Not because they want to micromanage, but because they're responsible for the bigger picture. Keeping them informed helps them advocate for resources, align with stakeholders, and keep the team on course.

But here's the catch: **not everything needs to be shared.** There's a fine line between being transparent and turning every meeting into a live feed of your thought process. Overcommunication can overwhelm, confuse, or even distract from what actually matters. Focus on providing relevant, timely updates that move the conversation forward.

The same principle applies in reverse. Managers should also be clear about expectations, shifting priorities, and any course corrections. Nothing demotivates a team faster than feeling blindsided by sudden changes, especially when they could've been flagged earlier.

Now let's talk about **escalation.** (No, not the dramatic kind.) We're talking about raising flags *before* things spiral out of control. When handled well, escalation isn't a sign of failure, it's a sign of maturity. It says,

"Hey, there's a storm on the horizon, and I'm not waiting to capsize before I ask for backup."

Great teams build clear, trusted pathways for flagging challenges. Everyone knows when to escalate, how to do it, and, most importantly that doing so won't get them punished. It's not about tattling. It's about building a culture where saying "I need help" is seen as a strength, not a weakness.

Managers play a key role here too. They must create space for honest dialogue, especially around setbacks. When team members trust that their leader won't overreact or shut them down, they're more likely to speak up early. And that early warning system? It's pure gold in fast- paced, high- stakes environments.

The Escalation Path

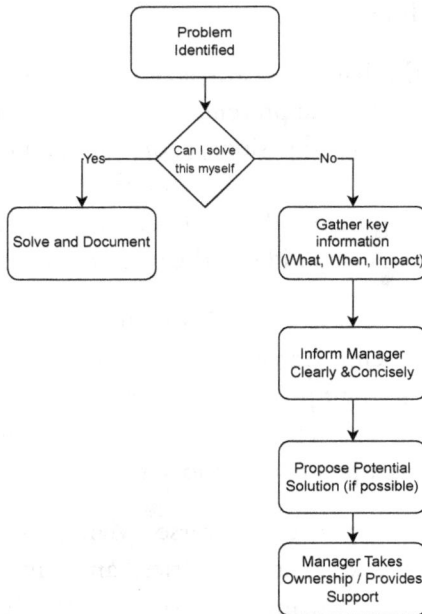

So, whether you're the one setting the direction or the one executing the plan, managing expectations boils down to this: **communicate clearly, escalate wisely, and treat transparency as a two way street.**

WESTERN PROFESSIONALISM BENGALI ROOTS

When everyone's on the same page, navigating the unexpected becomes just another part of the journey, not a detour to disaster.

Benefits of Escalation Processes:

Let's clear the air: escalation doesn't mean panic. It doesn't mean finger pointing. And it certainly doesn't mean you've failed. In high functioning teams, **escalation is a sign of health,** not dysfunction.

Here's why building and encouraging a thoughtful escalation process is one of the smartest things any manager or organization can do.

1. It Builds Trust-Not Drama

When team members feel safe raising red flags, something powerful happens: trust deepens. Escalation becomes a conversation, not a confrontation. Managers get insight into potential issues early while there's still time to do something about them. And team members stop fearing that asking for help will make them look incompetent.

In short: **everyone wins when no one's afraid to speak up.**

2. It Keeps Customers (and Managers) from Being Blindsided

Let's say a customer reported issue lands on your desk. It's tempting to hand it off and move on but the best teams know that **ownership matters.** Even if someone else is fixing it, the person who escalated it stays in the loop until resolution. That follow through ensures nothing gets lost in the shuffle and reinforces accountability across the board.

Escalation isn't just about passing the responsibility, it's about seeing it through to resolution.

3. It Clarifies Priorities and Prevents Ping - Pong Confusion

Without a clear escalation path, issues bounce around like a hot potato: "Not my problem. Maybe Marketing? IT? Legal?" That chaos is exhausting and it wastes time.

Smart teams define **who handles what.** Is this urgent? Strategic? Technical? Once priorities are in place, team members know exactly where to go. No guesswork. No drama. Just solutions.

4. It Encourages Real Ownership - Not Just Pass the Buck Culture

When escalation works well, it doesn't just funnel problems upward, it pulls people into the **solution process.** Team members take responsibility for seeing issues through, even when the fix is out of their direct control. That shift from "not my job" to "I've got this until it's done" creates a culture of ownership that spreads across the team.

And let's face it: people do their best work when they know their voice matters.

5. It Equips Teams to Act - Not Just React

An effective escalation process is only as strong as the people using it. That's why training matters. When team members are trained not just in *what* to escalate but *how* and *when*, they feel empowered to take appropriate action without hesitation.

Think of it like giving your team a playbook: they're not frozen when things go wrong, they're ready to make the right move.

6. It Fuels a Culture of Continuous Improvement

Every issue is a learning opportunity, *if* we take the time to reflect. Building feedback loops into the escalation process means the team doesn't just solve today's problem; they reduce the chances of tomorrow's.

When management treats escalations as data, not drama, it can refine workflows, close communication gaps, and tighten accountability. Over time, this makes the team sharper, more agile, and far more resilient.

Bottom Line: Escalation done right isn't just a safety valve, it's a strategic asset. It builds trust, fosters ownership, and gives your team the confidence to act when it matters most. Instead of hiding problems, you're surfacing them, fixing them, and learning as you go.

Now that's what healthy leadership looks like.

Managing the Wider Team

Gone are the days when being a "manager" meant watching over just your own team and occasionally reporting up the chain. Today's leaders manage *in all directions:* up to senior leadership, across to other teams, and sometimes, even out to a team member's home life. It's a full circle experience, and doing it well requires more than just good intentions. It takes communication savvy, emotional intelligence, and a clear understanding of how influence works in a modern workplace.

Let's discuss what that really looks like.

Upward Management: How to Lead Those Who Lead You

Yes, managing *up* is a real thing, and, no, it's not manipulation or flattery. It's about knowing when and how to **leverage senior leadership strategically.** Maybe you need help navigating roadblocks. Maybe your team needs resources. Or maybe you're trying to align a project with the bigger company vision. Whatever the case, upward delegation can't just be a complaint disguised as a request.

Instead, great managers learn to speak the language of results. They clearly outline what they need, why it matters, and what outcomes leadership can expect. It's about making it easy for your leaders to say yes, because you've already shown them the value.

And don't forget: managing up also means **building rapport**. Keep your leaders in the loop. Ask for feedback. Show respect, but don't shy away from bringing ideas to the table. That blend of communication and confidence gets noticed.

Cross - Team Collaboration: It's Not Optional

No team exists in a vacuum. Especially in large organizations, most goals require coordination across departments, marketing, ops, tech, finance, you name it.

That's why managers need to be part **diplomat**, part **project manager**, and part **negotiator**.

Here's how to do it well:

- **Set clear goals and boundaries** from the beginning.

- **Agree on deliverables and timelines** - and then hold each other accountable.

- **Keep communication lines open**, even when (especially when) things get messy.

Cross team collaboration isn't just about checking boxes. It's about finding alignment between different teams with different pressures, and still finding a way to deliver. This is most effective when managers can balance empathy with execution.

Managing Outward: Yes, Families Matter

Here's a truth too many leaders overlook: **Your team's lives don't end when they clock out.** Their families, routines, and personal lives directly impact how they show up at work.

Managers who recognize this, and act on it, build fierce loyalty.

That might mean:

- Offering flexible schedules during school exam weeks.

- Hosting family- friendly office events.

- Simply checking in during tough personal times.(e.g. bereavement)

These seemingly small gestures speak volumes, and they are the norm in the West. They say, "We see you. And we care." That kind of emotional safety creates teams who stick around and go the extra mile because they know they're not just a cog in the wheel.

Leading Temporary Teams: You Set the Tone

Whether you're spearheading a six week task force or leading a cross functional sprint, **your behavior becomes the template** for everyone else. If you bring energy, humility, and transparency to the table, your team will reflect it. If you show up defensive and dismissive, don't be surprised when collaboration crumbles.

Remember: **great leadership is caught, not just taught.** What you model matters more than what you mandate.

When the Tables Turn: Reporting to Someone on Your Team

Here is something you may not expect in Western culture: Every now and then, you might find yourself reporting to someone you usually manage, especially on project, based assignments or rotational leadership programs. And that's okay. In fact, **it's a brilliant opportunity to demonstrate humility** and model adaptability.

Support their leadership. Offer your strengths. And above all, resist the urge to micromanage from the back seat.

When leaders can be led, it sends a clear message: **we're all here to grow together.** Hierarchy doesn't matter as much as progress.

Managing Up is a Strategy
Effectively managing your senior leaders is a critical skill. Learn to leverage their experience and positions to gain resources, solve complex problems, and ensure your team's work is aligned with broader organizational goals.

Responsibility in Teams for Senior Managers

If leadership had a core muscle group, **responsibility would be the abs,** essential, constantly tested, and directly tied to strength and integrity. For senior managers, responsibility isn't just about making sure the work gets done. It's about shaping a culture where accountability isn't feared, it's embraced.

And let's be clear: responsibility is not about doing everything yourself. It's about making sure **the right things get done by the right people in the right way** and owning the consequences when they don't.

Leadership Means Owning the Bigger Picture

At this level, you're not just thinking about who's doing what. You're thinking about:

- The **impact of your decisions** on the company,

- The **health and motivation** of your team,

- And the **long term ripple effects** of your leadership choices.

Being responsible means stepping up, not just when things go right, but especially when they don't. It means acknowledging mistakes, learning from them, and setting a tone of transparency rather than blame.

Senior managers who are successful in the West often walk a tightrope: giving enough guidance to steer the ship, but enough space for the crew to navigate. The best leaders don't just manage, they **mentor, model, and mobilize.**

Defining the Scope: What Are You *Really* Responsible For?

If you try to own everything, you'll end up owning nothing. Clarity is your best friend.

Start by asking:

- What decisions must stay with me?

- What responsibilities can and should be delegated?

- Where do I need visibility vs. direct control?

By drawing clear lines around your scope of responsibility, you give yourself permission to lead from the right distance and your team permission to take full control of the project.

And don't forget: these boundaries should be flexible. Priorities change. Crises arise. Empowerment today might mean involvement tomorrow. Just be clear and communicative when those shifts happen.

Create a Culture Where Responsibility Feels Safe

The best kind of responsibility isn't heavy. It's **shared**.

That starts with building an environment where:

- People feel safe sharing ideas, challenges, and yes - mistakes.

- Everyone knows their role, their value, and their guardrails.

- Ownership is expected, celebrated, and supported.

You do this by setting expectations early and often. Host role - clarity sessions. Document responsibilities clearly. Review them when things change. The more visible these roles are, the easier it becomes for everyone to stay aligned.

And when your team members deliver? Recognize it. Publicly. Privately. Often. Because what gets celebrated, gets repeated, and praise is expected in the Western workplace.

Delegate without Disappearing

Let's bust a myth: **Delegation is not dumping.**

Delegation is a strategic decision to empower others, while still:

- Providing guidance,

- Offering support,

- And staying close enough to course - correct when needed.

It's not a situation where you just hand the work over and not think about it again. It's a balancing act - sometimes leading, sometimes following. The goal is autonomy, not abandonment.

Summary: Leading with Responsibility, Not Burden

Responsibility doesn't have to feel like a weight. When done well, it's what gives leadership **meaning, credibility, and direction**.

Great senior managers lead by example, define their scope clearly, foster open communication, and build teams where everyone is proud to own their part of the mission.

Because when responsibility is shared with trust, not fear? That's when teams thrive, and legacies are built.

Delegate Problems, Not Just Tasks

Don't just assign tasks; empower your team with the autonomy to solve complex problems. Trusting in their professional judgment not only enhances efficiency but also fosters a powerful sense of ownership and accountability.

Communication Strategies

Let's face it, in the Western **modern workplace, communication is a jungle gym**. You've got emails, Slack, phone calls, Teams, WhatsApp, and the occasional sticky note left on your chair. Each tool has its moment, and you must master knowing when to use it.

So, how do you choose the right tool without accidentally sending a novel via instant message or calling someone in the middle of their weekly yoga retreat?

Let's break it down:

Instant Messaging: **The Quick Ping**

Think of instant messaging as the **office hallway wave**, quick, informal, but still polite.

- Use it for non urgent questions or updates that need a response within a few hours.

- Be brief. You're not writing a poem, unless your manager appreciates that kind of flair.

- A quick "Hi [Name], hope you're doing well" before jumping into your question never hurts.

And, yes, **emojis are okay**, if your team uses them. If they don't, maybe save that dancing avocado for your group chat.

Email: The Professional Workhorse

Email is your **digital briefcase,** clean, structured, and made for important or detailed information.

- Use it for formal requests, detailed updates, or anything that should be documented.

- Emails are perfect for issues that can wait a day or two.

- Subject lines should be clear, not cryptic. For example: "Project Update – Q3 Launch Plan" beats "Hey."

Tone matters. When in doubt, **go formal, not frantic**.

- "Dear" still works.

- "Sincerely" is classy.

- "Thanks" is always welcome, especially if someone saved your deadline from imploding.

Pro tip: Do a quick proofread before hitting send. Typos are sneaky little things.

Phone Calls: The Fast Track

Sometimes, you just need to pick up the phone.

- If it's complex, urgent, or emotionally nuanced, **call**.

- Don't ambush. Check if it's a good time.

- Be clear about your purpose right away. You're not trying to sell a vacuum cleaner.

Bonus: With a phone call, you can hear tone and nuance, which makes a world of difference when handling sensitive or layered topics.

Communicating Through Assistants

Scheduling a meeting with someone who's always booked solid? **Their assistant is your new best friend.**

- Be courteous, clear, and respectful. They are gatekeepers, not messengers.

- Provide everything they need upfront: names, dates, purpose, and contact details.

- And, no, you're not "just" speaking to an assistant. You're engaging with a member of their professional team. Treat them as such.

General Communication Etiquette: Observe the Tone of the Environment (and the Culture)

Professional communication is like fashion, **context is everything.**

- In formal situations or unfamiliar relationships, stay formal and polite.

- With closer colleagues, a more relaxed tone might be fine, but always respectful.

- Unsure about pronouns? Just ask. Or better yet, use their name until you know for sure.

Even your sign off matters. Here's your cheat sheet:

- **"Sincerely"** = formal, respectful, ideal for first timers.

- **"Kind regards"** = versatile, warm, still professional.

- **"Thanks"** or **"Thank you"** = helpful, collaborative, and always appreciated.

WESTERN PROFESSIONALISM BENGALI ROOTS

Summary: Communicate Like a Pro

In short: **know your tools, respect your audience, and match your message to the moment.** Great communicators aren't loud or flashy they're thoughtful, timely, and clear.

Because in today's workplace, it's not just about *what* you say, it's *how* you deliver it.

Understanding Stake holders (Internal and External)

Who's Watching and Why It Matters

If you've ever tried to plan a surprise birthday party only to realize halfway through that someone forgot to invite Grandma, the one funding the whole event, you've felt the sting of **stakeholder oversight**.

Now imagine that same misstep, but at work, where missed stakeholders don't just feel left out, but can derail your entire project.

In the professional world, understanding who your stakeholders are and what they care about, isn't optional. It's essential. Especially when it comes to managing **escalations**. These are the moments when things heat up and everyone suddenly wants to know what's going on.

So, let's map the territory.

Direct vs. Indirect Stakeholders

Not everyone wears a project manager badge or signs off on deliverables, but that doesn't mean they don't matter.

- **Direct stakeholders** are your frontline folks: teammates, managers, and clients who are directly involved.

- **Indirect stakeholders** might seem out of the loop, until your project bumps into their priorities. These include people like departments impacted by your timeline, support teams, or external partners with skin in the game.

If their world could shift based on what you do (or don't do), **they fit into this category.**

Influence vs. Interest

Stakeholders are not created equal.

Some have power but little day to day concern. Others care deeply but have little pull. A few have **both influence and interest.** These are your top tier folks. Keep them close and keep them updated.

Here's the rule of thumb:

- High **influence**, high **interest** = communicate often, clearly, and with detail.

- Low **interest**, low **influence** = don't flood their inbox. A light touch will do.

The Stakeholder Matrix

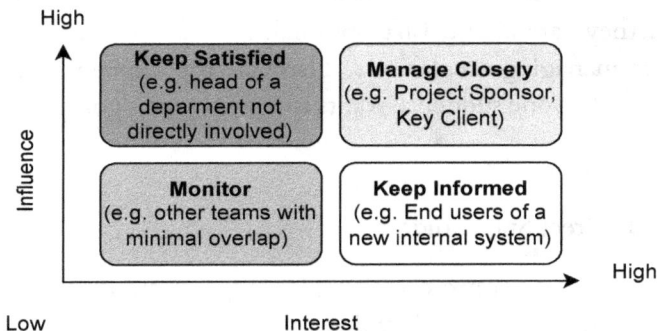

Stakeholder Communication Strategy

If you want your project to breathe easy during tense moments, **perfect your communication game**. Here's how:

Customized Communication

No one wants to read a novella when a quick note will do, or worse, get ignored when they needed answers.

Match your message to the person.
For a busy executive, use bullet points and bottom lines.
For a curious team member, provide background and clarity. Always keep your message **relevant**, **accessible**, and **respectfully tailored**.

Transparency Builds Trust

Even when the news isn't great, honesty wins. Tell stakeholders:

- What's happening

- What you're doing about it

- What they can expect next

You'll head off rumors and reduce surprise escalations. In other words, by communicating consistently, **you control the narrative.**

Proactive Beats Reactive

Don't wait for people to come knocking. Set a rhythm for updates. Weekly emails, dashboards, or quick stand ups all work, just make it predictable.

When stakeholders know when they'll hear from you, they're less likely to fill in the blanks with guesses and worst case scenarios.

Build in Feedback Loops

Give stakeholders a voice. Ask:

- "Does this update meet your needs?"

- "Are there any concerns we've missed?"

Their feedback helps you adjust your strategy, make better decisions, and deepen the relationship.

Centralized and Consistent

Ever had five people working off five different versions of "the plan"? Not fun.

Use a shared platform or system, whether that's a dashboard, shared folder, or internal portal, to house project updates and escalation details. That way, everyone accesses the same truth.

Mind the Confidentiality

Not all details are for all eyes. You can share progress and challenges **without giving out sensitive, private specifics**. Know your audience, protect privacy, and still keep people looped in where it counts.

Protocols Keep You Sane

When escalation hits, you want to have a plan in place. Have clear answers to:

- Who needs to know?
- When should they know it?
- How much detail is necessary?

Define the **who, what, and when** ahead of time, and you'll move from chaos to confidence.

Final Thought

Every stakeholder is a valuable part of your project. The best professionals know how to keep all stakeholders in the know, with empathy, precision, and a well- timed update.

How to Handle the "Uh - Oh" Moments Like a Pro

Let's be honest **mistakes are inevitable**. Even the most flawless professionals spill coffee on reports, send the wrong file, or completely misjudge a timeline. It's not about avoiding mistakes entirely; it's about how we respond when they happen. And that response? It's a direct reflection of leadership maturity.

Here's how to turn those cringeworthy moments into catalysts for growth.

Proactive Planning: The Best Time to Prepare for a Mistake Is Before It Happens

Great managers don't just hope nothing goes wrong. They **plan for the possibility** that it will.

By laying out clear processes and creating space for quick reporting, they make it easier for team members to:

- Catch errors early

- Flag them without fear

- Correct them swiftly

With a proactive mindset, the team knows what to do when mistakes arise and most importantly, they know it's okay to speak up.

Understand the Significance and Impact

Not every mistake is a crisis.

Part of good management is knowing the difference in importance between a typo in an internal note and a data breach that affects external clients

Before reacting, pause to assess:

- What's the damage?

- Who's affected?

- What's the ripple effect?

This insight helps you **prioritize your response**, tailor your communication, and pick the right level of urgency for recovery.

Damage Control: When Mistakes Matter, Here's What to Do

Once you've gauged the weight of the mistake, damage control is about executing a smart, well paced plan, not panicking.

1. **Take Immediate Action**

Contain the situation. Fix the visible error. If needed, deploy a backup plan. Don't wait - **act decisively**.

2. **Be Transparent with Stakeholders**

Don't spin, deflect, or delay. Stakeholders appreciate clarity:

- What happened

- What you're doing about it

- What comes next

This transparency **builds trust**, even in tough moments.

3. **Learn and Prevent**

Every mistake carries a lesson. Don't waste it.

- Investigate the root cause

- Document it

- Adjust your process, training, or structure

The goal isn't just to clean up the mess it's to **make sure it doesn't happen again**.

Fostering a Positive Post - Mistake Environment

Mistakes can bruise egos and morale. That's why how you **lead afterward** matters most.

Accountability Over Blame

Replace blame and shame with learning. When leaders take responsibility openly, it gives everyone else permission to do the same. Blame kills creativity. Accountability builds resilience.

Emotional Support

Mistakes are stressful. Be the kind of leader who **sees the human side** of error. Support your team. Let them process. Then help them move forward stronger.

Collective Ownership

Even if just one person made the mistake, it likely happened within a broader system. Frame it as a **team issue**. This encourages unity and constructive dialogue instead of shame.

Reward the Fix

When someone steps up to fix a mistake or catches it early, celebrate that. It shows that solutions matter more than setbacks, and it creates a culture of initiative.

Debrief and Rebuild Confidence

Run a no blame debrief:

- What did we learn?

- What will we do differently next time?

- How can we support each other moving forward?

Then, offer encouragement. Reaffirm strengths. Let your team know this one mistake doesn't define their value.

Apologies and Mistake Ownership: Get It Right

An apology isn't a legal defense or a speech about good intentions. It's about **owning the impact** of your actions with humility and care.

- Say what went wrong

- Acknowledge how it affected others

- Show empathy

- Then - only after you can offer a solution

A good apology **doesn't justify**, it connects. It humanizes you. It builds trust.

Impact of a Mistake

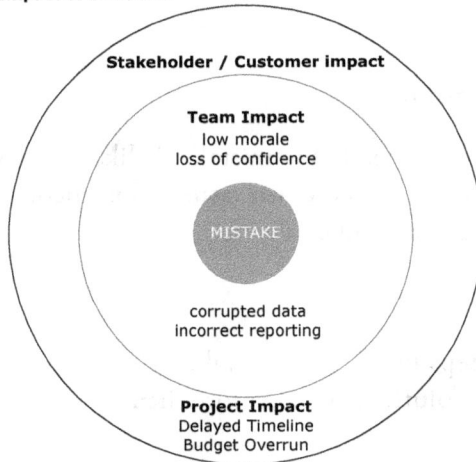

Stakeholder / Customer impact

Team Impact
low morale
loss of confidence

MISTAKE

corrupted data
incorrect reporting

Project Impact
Delayed Timeline
Budget Overrun

Final Word

Mistakes are uncomfortable, but they're also powerful. When handled with transparency, grace, and strategy, they become **milestones of growth** rather than scars of failure.

And in the long run, how you lead through a mistake will teach your team more than any perfect day ever could.

CHAPTER 8:
A BRIDGE WORTH BUILDING

As we bring this guide to a close, let's take a breath, not to say we're done, but to mark the beginning of something richer. What lies ahead for you as a Bangladeshi professional working in Western contexts isn't just a career journey, it's a personal evolution. But don't shed your identity, own it, use it to your benefit, and sharpen it. Your Bengali roots will be a superpower in the Western culture, not a stumbling block.

In this global landscape, where Zoom calls stretch across time zones and lunch meetings mix curries with croissants, your focus now is to master your soft skills. This will be the key to your success. This book has been your guide for doing so, offering you an opportunity for growth, confidence, and impact.

The Power of Self Awareness

It all starts with you.

Not the polished résumé version. Not even the most fluent, LinkedIn approved, English - speaking you. But the honest, curious version who's willing to ask: "Why do I do it this way?" That's where the real transformation begins.

Maybe you've noticed that your sense of hierarchy or how you say sorry or don't, comes from something deeper. Maybe you've realized that your sense of urgency or your reaction to feedback isn't just personal, it's cultural.

That's powerful knowledge. And once you see it, you can shift it. You can pause, pivot, and approach situations with intentionality instead of defaulting to habit. That's not losing your culture. That's leading with it.

Building Bridges Through Communication

By now, you've seen that communication is more than grammar and vocabulary. It's a balance of the spoken and unspoken, tone, timing, and cultural politeness.

You've learned that directness, transparency, and expectation - setting are cornerstones of Western professional life. But you've also learned something deeper: that listening, humility, and kindness are accepted across all cultural lines.

Even the smallest words, "please," "thanks," "I understand", can build trust faster than credentials ever could. When used well, these tools don't just help you succeed; they help you connect.

Fostering an Inclusive Mindset

Let's not sugarcoat it: the workplace, any workplace, can carry bias.

Sometimes it shows up as ageism, or assumptions based on gender. Sometimes it's subtle, like who gets to speak first in a meeting or whose ideas are taken seriously. You've explored how these issues show up in both Bangladeshi and Western contexts.

Now, you have the language and awareness to navigate them on your own not with anger or fear, but with confidence and clarity. You're not just there to participate. You're there to shape the space. And as someone who lives within two different cultures, you have a unique role to play in making those spaces more fair, more aware, and more human.

A Call to Action: Lifelong Learning and Growth

Here's the secret: you never really "arrive."

Cultural competence isn't something you earn once and get a certificate. It's a lifelong practice, a mindset of growth, humility, and curiosity.

You'll make mistakes. You'll get it wrong. And if you're paying attention, you'll also get better.

Ask for feedback. Reflect often. Seek out perspectives that stretch your own. Be open to shifting the way you lead, listen, and learn. Because when you do, you're not just keeping pace with the global workplace, you're setting the pace.

A Final Word: You Are the Bridge

Every company, every project, every team needs someone who can bridge worlds. Someone who gets the nuance, who translates not just words but values. Someone who knows how to navigate the stormy parts of cultural difference with grace, humor, and humanity.

You can be that person.

You've got the roots. You've got the range. And now, you've got the roadmap.

So go out there. Lead well. Learn deeply. And carry your culture not as a burden, but as a beacon.

Because the world doesn't just need more global professionals.

It needs a more global you.

Curiosity Over Judgment

When encountering a cultural practice you don't understand, approach it with curiosity. Asking respectful questions or observing with an open mind prevents misinterpretation and builds stronger, more authentic relationships across diverse teams.

APPENDIX 1: THE PRACTICALITIES OF THE WESTERN JOB HUNT

Before you can dazzle colleagues in a cross cultural brainstorming session or charm clients in the West with your inclusive leadership style, there's one tiny detail to address: **you need the job first.**

Applying to Western companies can feel like stepping into a completely different universe, where cover letters need to be detailed but concise, résumés need to stand out (but not too much), and interviews often involve questions that feel a little too intrusive.

But don't worry. This section is your insider guide to decoding the rituals of the Western job market. From crafting a standout résumé to surviving that final round interview, we'll walk through the essentials that help get your foot not just in the door, but in the right door.

1. Crafting Your CV/Resume for a Western Audience

Let's start with a reality check: **Your resume isn't your life story.** It's your elevator pitch on paper.

In many countries, resumes can run long, include personal details, and read like a memoir. In the West, particularly in the US, UK, Canada, and Australia, your resume should be laser focused, achievement packed, and tailored for the job you're applying for. Think of it like your personal ad campaign, and you're the product.

Here's how to make yours stand out:

- **Keep It Concise.**
  Recruiters spend *seconds* skimming resumes. Aim for **two pages max**, or just **one page** if you're early in your career. That's not a limit, it's an opportunity to cut the fluff and keep only what sells.

- **Leave Out Personal Details.**
  No photo. No birthday. No marital status. No nationality. Western resumes are stripped of anything that could lead to bias. Including these details can actually hurt your chances because companies have to protect themselves from discrimination claims.

- **Show What You Achieved – Not Just What You Did.**
  Think results, not responsibilities. Instead of:

  "Responsible for managing the project budget…"

  Say:

  "Managed a £50,000 budget, delivering the project 10% under budget through strategic vendor negotiations."

Every bullet point should start with a strong action verb and end with something measurable or meaningful.

- **Quantify Everything You Can.**
  Numbers talk. They prove you've done the work and delivered results. Did you increase sales? Cut costs? Speed up delivery time? Say so. If you can back it up with percentages, even better.

- **Tailor Your Resume for Every Application.**
  Yes, every one. A generic resume looks like you're just clicking "Apply All." Study the job description. Mirror the language they use. If they want "client engagement experience," make sure your resume *says* "client engagement experience." Small tweaks show big interest.

> **Your Resume is a Marketing Document**
> In the West, a resume's only job is to get you an interview. It's not
> a complete life history. Focus on quantifiable achievements over
> job duties, and tailor it to each specific role you apply for.

2. Mastering the Western Interview: The STAR Method

Think of a Western job interview like a first date with high stakes. It's less about proving your genius and more about showing how well you think, adapt, and play with others. Yes, your technical knowledge matters, but what really gets noticed is how you handle real-life situations.

That's where **behavioral interview questions** come in. You'll hear phrases like:

"Tell me about a time when you had to work under pressure . . ."
"Describe a situation where you disagreed with a teammate . . ."
"Give an example of a time you made a mistake . . ."

Sound familiar? These questions are designed to peel back the surface and find out what kind of colleague you really are when things get tough, messy, or unpredictable.

Enter the STAR method. It's your go to formula for telling stories that highlight your skills - without rambling or going off track.

The STAR Breakdown:

- **S – Situation**
  Set the scene. Where were you? What was going on? Keep it short, just enough context so they can follow the story.

- **T – Task**
  What was your goal? What were *you* supposed to do? Make this part personal. They want to know your specific responsibility.

- **A – Action**
  This is the heart of the story. What steps did you take to solve the problem? Use "I" statements, not "we." Even in a team, you need

to spotlight your contribution. Be specific and logical, walk them through your thought process.

- **R – Result**
  What happened? Did things improve? Did you learn something? Did you save the day? Try to quantify your results: "We finished the project 2 weeks early," "Customer satisfaction increased by 25%," "I was promoted because of it." End on a strong, reflective note. **Real - Life** Example:

Question: *"Tell me about a time you faced a conflict with a colleague."*

S – Situation:

"In my previous role, a senior colleague and I had a disagreement about the technical direction for a new product feature. We were stuck in a stalemate, and it was holding up the entire team."

T – Task:

"I needed to resolve the conflict and help the team move forward with a solution that was both effective and maintainable."

A – Action:

"I invited my colleague for a one - on - one conversation to understand his point of view. I listened without interrupting, then presented my own idea, along with a working prototype I'd built to demonstrate the benefits. I made it clear that I wasn't trying to 'win' the debate, but to find the best path for the project."

R – Result:

"He appreciated the effort and evidence, and we ended up merging the best parts of both our ideas. The feature launched on time, and our relationship actually improved, we later collaborated on two other major projects without any friction."

> **The STAR Method: Your Interview Superpower**
> When answering behavioral questions, use the STAR Method to structure your story:
> - **Situation**: Set the scene.
> - **Task**: Describe your goal.
> - **Action**: Detail the steps **you** took.
> - **Result**: Explain the positive outcome. This technique provides a clear, compelling, and memorable narrative of your accomplishments.

3. The Art of Professional Networking

If you've ever heard someone say, "It's not what you know, it's who you know," you've already met the Western job market's not - so - secret ingredient: **networking**.

But let's clear something up: networking is not begging for a job. It's not awkward small talk over stale coffee. And it's definitely not reserved for extroverts or executives. At its heart, networking is about building genuine relationships-before you need them.

In many Western countries, jobs are often passed along through whispers before they hit the job boards. Those who are already connected are first in line.

So how do you get there? Here are some tips:

Leverage LinkedIn **Like a Pro**

Think of LinkedIn as your virtual business card, resume, portfolio, and elevator pitch - all in one. It's your digital handshake.

- Fill it out completely: Photo. Headline. About section. Work experience.

- Match your resume: Recruiters cross check. Be consistent.

- Be visible: Share articles. Comment on posts. Celebrate others' successes.

➤ Grow your network: Connect with former classmates, colleagues, and new contacts from conferences or webinars.

Try Informational Interviews

One of the most powerful (and underused) strategies? Asking someone for twenty minutes of their time to learn about their job, not to ask for one.

- Send a thoughtful message: Be clear you're looking for insight, not employment.

- Be curious, not transactional: Ask about their career path, challenges, advice.

- Follow up with thanks: Gratitude goes far in any culture.

You'll gain insider knowledge - and possibly a future ally.

Give Before You Ask

True networking is reciprocal. It's not a one-way street where you constantly ask for favors.

- Can you connect two people with similar interests?

- Can you share an article someone might find valuable?

- Can you show support by liking and commenting on their content?

In fact, this approach beautifully mirrors a strength found in Bangladeshi culture: generosity. When applied professionally, it builds trust, credibility, and a lasting reputation.

The Bigger Picture: Your Career, Your Legacy

I've been fortunate to have a long career in leadership, and let me be honest: I didn't write this guide because everything has gone smoothly. I wrote it because I've seen too much potential wasted over small but costly mistakes. I've watched Western professionals walk away from brilliant Bangladeshi and Indian colleagues simply because they didn't understand the unspoken rules.

And I've faced bias myself, not always the aggressive, obvious kind, but also the quiet assumptions about your age, your background, or your worth.

But here's what I've learned: life offers us windows, moments when the right mindset, the right skills, and the right opportunity align. And those windows don't stay open forever.1

So build your network, yes but also build your vision. Create a growth plan that isn't limited to your current job title or paycheck. Because a salary can be a blessing but it can also become a leash, tying you to someone else's dream while yours waits in the background.

You were made for more. This guide has been about equipping you with the tools to walk confidently into global opportunities, communicate with clarity and grace, and lead with both skill and humility. Now, the next move is yours.

A Little Note about AI

For a lot of professionals, AI is a game-changer and definitely a risk to our careers if we don't harness and take advantage of it.

It's also why our experience is incredibly more important than ever before. Without our guidance, AI solutions will not work. Our expertise enables us to recognise when things are going wrong and gain a deeper understanding of the larger picture. So, focus on developing your experience and accelerating it with the use of AI.

AI is also useful for advising you on complex social contexts. I know I have used it several times to get out of sticky situations. Alongside the knowledge from this book and a little help from AI, you can steer discussions appropriately.

www.ingramcontent.com/pod-product-compliance
Lightning Source LLC
Chambersburg PA
CBHW071705210326
41597CB00017B/2341